Praise for L

Whether you are considering a ro
leader or looking to go further
Leading Maths provides invaluabl
with a range of relevant issues fro
complex themes around challenges within teams. Although more secondary leaning, advice and suggestions are applicable to primary and Mattock references these where possible. The whole tone of *Leading Maths* is conversational, clear and allows one to feel supported. Advice is sensible and, because it is based on experiences of Mattock and others via case studies, feels adaptable and actionable for any setting. Overall, *Leading Maths* is a vital read for anyone in maths leadership.

Lisa Coe, former Trust-wide Primary Maths Lead

Even with 10+ years' leadership experience this book gave me some insights on how to improve my leadership skills, and probably helped me understand why I had failed to secure some roles in the past! This book has something for everyone, whether you are leading a department, aspiring to have a leadership role, are a line manager for maths or someone who just wants a better understanding of the challenges faced by the leader of maths.

**David Faram, Director of Learning (Mathematics),
The Trinity School**

This book is packed full of helpful advice for a head of maths. Drawing extensively on the author's personal experience, *Leading Maths* provides guidance on the day-to-day operational aspects of the role, as well as the more strategic side of department leadership. It features practical research-informed ideas for managing and developing staff, dealing with difficult situations, covering absences, curriculum planning, assessment, recruitment, inspections and much more. This book will be of great value to any new or aspiring maths leader.

Jo Morgan, Head of Maths, writer of *resourceaholic.com* and author of *A Compendium of Mathematical Methods*

A very useful and informative reference book for new and experienced heads of maths. What Peter Mattock has created is incredible. A definitive insight for leaders in mathematics. The role of a leader in maths is challenging and demanding. This book aims to provide a roadmap to help you focus your attention on areas that will have the biggest impact, as well as giving you helpful ideas on the soft skills that are involved in leading a large team of teachers. I wish I had this book 10 years ago!

**Kapilesh Nagar, Head of Mathematics,
Moat Community College**

Peter Mattock

Leading Maths

The essential guide for new and aspiring maths leaders

Crown House Publishing Limited
www.crownhouse.co.uk

First published by
Crown House Publishing Limited
Crown Buildings, Bancyfelin, Carmarthen, Wales, SA33 5ND, UK
www.crownhouse.co.uk

and

Crown House Publishing Company LLC
PO Box 2223, Williston, VT 05495, USA
www.crownhousepublishing.com

© Peter Mattock and Crown House Publishing, 2023.

The right of Peter Mattock to be identified as the author of this work has been asserted by him in accordance with the Copyright, Designs and Patents Act 1988.

Cover images © vectorplus– stock.adobe.com.

All rights reserved. Except as permitted under current legislation no part of this work may be photocopied, stored in a retrieval system, published, performed in public, adapted, broadcast, transmitted, recorded or reproduced in any form or by any means, without the prior permission of the copyright owners. Enquiries should be addressed to Crown House Publishing.

Crown House Publishing has no responsibility for the persistence or accuracy of URLs for external or third-party websites referred to in this publication, and does not guarantee that any content on such websites is, or will remain, accurate or appropriate.

First published 2023.

British Library Cataloguing-in-Publication Data

A catalogue entry for this book is available from the British Library.

Print ISBN 978-178583697-8
Mobi ISBN 978-178583699-2
ePub ISBN 978-178583700-5
ePDF ISBN 978-178583701-2

LCCN 2023939801

Printed and bound in the UK by
Charlesworth Press, Wakefield, West Yorkshire

Acknowledgements

My last two books have had very personal dedications to my (now) wife, Rowan; my mum, Lesley; my children, Erin and Mollie; my grandparents, Ted, Alan, June and Patricia; and my closest friends in the world, Chris, John and Paul. You all remain loved and appreciated for the joy and support you have brought me. Without all of you, I wouldn't have got anywhere near to where I am today.

But the dedication for this book is slightly different. This is to all of the maths leaders and aspiring maths leaders out there. Driving forwards the teaching and learning of mathematics that our pupils receive is an incredibly important job. As I write this, the landscape of education in the UK is making this an increasingly difficult job. For anyone who takes it on in any capacity, no matter whether you ultimately feel successful at it or not, whether you do it for just a few years and then decide it isn't for you or whether you make an entire career out of it, your hard work and effort should never go unrecognised or unrewarded. I am not in a position to reward you, but I do recognise the challenges you face.

Of course, I need to say a special thank you to Becky Lawrence, Rhiannon Rainbow, Jemma Sherwood and Dave Tushingham who have gifted their knowledge and experience alongside my own in the composition of this work. Your contributions are greatly and warmly received, and my deepest appreciations go to the four of you.

Contents

Acknowledgements i

Introduction 1

Chapter 1   Getting the job 7
                     Interviews 10
                     School tours 16
                     Observed lessons 17
                     Data tasks 17
                     Lesson observations 18
                     Key points 19

Chapter 2   Getting stuck in 21
                     Quick wins 21
                     Time management 23
                     Behaviour and practice 26
                     Leadership style 29
                     Getting to know your team 32
                     Key points 35

Chapter 3   Day-to-day management 37
                     Managing behaviour 37
                     Covering absences 39
                     Monitoring 42
                     Admin 43
                     Key points 46

Chapter 4   Strategic leadership 47
                     Curriculum planning 47
                     Assessment 51
                     Feedback and marking 58
                     Maths in other areas of the curriculum 60
                     Key points 61

Chapter 5   Subject time and development 63
                     Underperforming staff 68
                     Key points 70

Chapter 6	Dealing with results	71
	Responding to poor results	74
	Key points	77

Chapter 7	Difficult situations	79
	The uncooperative teacher	79
	Personal issues	81
	Split classes	83
	The management of non-specialist staff	85
	Key points	86

Chapter 8	Adding to your team	89
	Appointing teachers	92
	Appointing to leadership roles	93
	Key points	94

Chapter 9	Ofsted and inspections	97
	The deep dive	99
	Preparation	101
	Inspection day	103
	Key points	104

Chapter 10	Subject improvement plans and action planning	105
	Self-evaluation	108
	Key points	112

Chapter 11	Appraising others	113
	Barriers to progression	116
	Key points	119

| Chapter 12 | Leading beyond your school | 121 |
| | Key points | 127 |

Chapter 13	Messages from other maths leaders	129
	Leading maths in a primary school	129
	Leading maths across a trust	133
	Key points	136
	Maths leadership	136
	Key points	140
	Summary	140

References *141*

Introduction

I am under no illusion; I have been incredibly lucky in my career so far. For the most part, the decisions I have made have worked out (and even the one that might not have been considered to work has taught me something). I have been in the right place at the right time to take up several opportunities. I have worked with excellent colleagues who have given me the benefit of their experience and led excellent staff who were open and adaptable to the changes I wanted to make. I have managed to find environments and surround myself with people who have a similar educational philosophy to my own, both in general and specifically in relation to mathematics (at least, for the time I have had a philosophy on such things). As with any career, particularly those in education, there have been ups and downs along the way – some of which can hopefully be avoided by others when they read this.

I trained to teach at the University of Leicester in 2005 and 2006 and took my first job as a maths teacher in July 2006 at Fitzharrys School in Abingdon, Oxfordshire. Fitzharrys was (and still is) a 'good' 11–18 school with relatively stable staffing and an intake that was predominantly white working and middle class. I am forever grateful to Dr Susan Tranter and the staff at Fitzharrys for starting my contract before the end of the school year, which allowed me to orient myself prior to my first full year and meet some of the pupils I would teach the following year (including my new form group on the Year 7 induction days), which meant I could spend my summer holiday preparing for my first classes rather than having to take a temporary job to keep the bills paid. I understand why this practice has become less prevalent in the years of tightened budgets, but I think this is a shame as I know how valuable it was for me as a newly qualified teacher.

When I first got to Fitzharrys, I became particularly interested in working with what were termed at the time 'gifted and talented' pupils. I read copious amounts of research by authors like Janet Bates, Sarah Munday and Dr Barry Hymer (helped by a membership of the education library at the University of Oxford) and even started an MA in gifted and talented education (which unfortunately I had to cut short when I took my first head of department role). Within a couple of years, I was recognised as a lead teacher in this area and was supporting the development of other teachers in working with gifted and talented pupils. I also began running professional development for initial teacher education (ITE) students at the invite of my PGCE mentor, Dr Geoff Tennant, initially at the University of Leicester and then at the University of Reading when he moved to a role there as senior lecturer for secondary maths ITE.

For the beginning of my third year at Fitz, I took my first maths leadership role as second-in-charge with particular responsibilities for the Key Stage 5 curriculum and outcomes as well as the use of ICT in maths and formally mentoring ITE trainees (I had done some co-mentoring with another member of the department prior to this). I kept this role for a little over a year, and then in January 2011, I took my first head of department role at the newly created Oxford Spires Academy in Blackbird Leys, an area in the south of the city of Oxford.

Oxford Spires Academy was different from Fitzharrys in virtually every way. Although a 'new' academy, it was replacing Oxford School which had only recently emerged from the National Challenge.[1] The school had seen a reasonable amount of staff turnover and served an ethnically diverse community with high levels of deprivation and disadvantage. The new academy was very effective in addressing the progress and attainment issues of its predecessor, and it is still one of the periods of my career of which I am most proud; in my first full year at the school, we achieved what were (and I believe still are) the highest maths results in the school's (or its predecessor's) history. This was recognised during an Ofsted visit the following January (2013), which was very complimentary about the maths department, including this comment: 'Students make particularly impressive progress in English and mathematics, often exceeding expected rates of progress, compared with students in similar schools.'[2]

It was during my time at Oxford Spires that I was able to take up a number of opportunities that extended my knowledge and experience of education. I co-ran a coaching programme for teachers, I sat on the board for ITE at both Oxford University and Oxford Brookes University, and I even ran ITE for a year at the school whilst the assistant head teacher, who was normally in charge of ITE placement students, had a leave of absence. All these experiences taught

---

[1] A. W. Darzi, *Schools: National Challenge*. HL Deb (10 June 2008), vol. 702. Available at: https://hansard.parliament.uk/Lords/2008-06-10/debates/08061086000008/SchoolsNationalChallenge.

[2] Ofsted, School Report: Oxford Spires Academy (9–10 July 2013). Available at: https://files.ofsted.gov.uk/v1/file/2263369.

me various lessons about leadership in general (which I will discuss in later chapters). However, I think the one opportunity that shaped my views on maths more than any other was the chance to produce professional development videos for the Key Stage 3 section of the ActivTeach platform from Pearson in and around 2013. It was here that I first came across the concrete-pictorial-abstract approach to mathematics education, which would spark my interest in the use of representations and manipulatives and would shape the latter half of my career to date, both in terms of my own practice and philosophy as well as how I have set up my departments and steered my team's development.

Due to my family's relocation back to the Midlands, I left Oxford Spires to take a role as director of mathematics, business and ICT at Nuneaton Academy in January 2014, my first role in an extended leadership team. Nuneaton Academy was simultaneously like a mix of both my previous schools and like nothing else I have ever experienced! The school had the high deprivation of Oxford Spires alongside the majority white ethnicity of Fitzharrys. However, what Nuneaton Academy taught me (in the short time I was there) was that without strong leadership from the top, particularly around expectations and behaviour, schools simply don't function well. Although I don't regret leaving after such a short time, as my next position was the defining role in my career, I do look back and wonder whether I could have been part of the transformation that the school needed to undergo (and I am pleased to say seems to have undergone in the intervening years).

And so, in August 2014, I started my role as director of learning for mathematics and numeracy at my current school, Brockington College in Leicestershire. Although ostensibly quite similar to Fitzharrys (less than average deprivation and majority white ethnicity, although only 11–14 at the time and 11–16 now), the challenges were completely different (and not just because I didn't actually lead the mathematics department at Fitz).

At the time I joined Brocko, it was a high school, taking pupils at age 11 and sending them on to an upper school at age 14. However, the school was transitioning (along with most of Leicestershire) from a high school/upper school model to a straight-through secondary model. My first year was the last year that the school was to be an 11–14 school; instead of sending the 14-year-olds off to an upper school that year we would keep them on to become the school's first Year 10. This meant that a big part of the early years of my role were spent designing and implementing the curriculum for 14–16, as well as recruiting and embedding the extra staff the department would need as it transitioned to 11–16.

Although I had done some curriculum planning at Oxford Spires, this was my first real experience of designing a coherent experience for pupils over a significant time span. It was also somewhat backwards, due to the nature of the transition; I think most people would prefer to start curriculum development chronologically, and so begin with age 11 and work up to age 16 (we will explore curriculum planning and development further in Chapter 4), but we had to focus very much on the 14–16 curriculum first, before going back to the 11–14 curriculum.

It was at Brockington College that I first got involved with the National Centre for Excellence in the Teaching of Mathematics,[3] first gaining my accreditation as a professional development lead and then training in the first cohort as a secondary teaching for mastery specialist, leading to becoming the secondary teaching for mastery lead for the East Midlands South Maths Hub. Combined with my work as a specialist leader in education, this was a great opportunity to work with schools and practitioners across the East Midlands and help to plan for their development.

Leading maths at any school is a unique challenge. Being a 'core' subject comes with pressures that are unlike many other subject areas. In addition, the relatively abstract nature of the subject content combined with the contrasting societal and often parental attitudes can make mathematics a Marmite subject; whilst all pupils recognise its importance (those who say they don't care invariably mean that either they struggle with it or they are so disengaged with school in general that their attitude isn't subject specific), it is simultaneously quite acceptable to be 'not good at maths'. Leading a subject area in schools is often about managing what seem at face value to be contradictions, and nowhere is this truer than in leading maths.[4]

Many volumes have been written about leadership, both in general and specifically in education. Huge amounts of research have been conducted into the most effective leadership styles; programmes

---

3   See https://www.ncetm.org.uk.
4   I have written about being a new head of department in: P. Mattock, Ten Steps to Surviving as a New Head of Department, *TES* (21 May 2017). Available at: https://www.tes.com/magazine/archive/ten-steps-surviving-new-head-department.

Introduction

allowing people to determine their leadership style are abundant. Books and guides on leading at all levels are readily available in all formats. It isn't my intention to rehash this research or advice (although I may touch on it on occasion). What does appear to be lacking is detailed advice and guidance on how to approach leadership in specific subject areas. This is what I am hoping to address in this book – to take the lessons learned from nearly 15 years in maths leadership and explore the challenges and rewards that come with this position.

We will start by looking at how we actually secure a role in maths leadership, before moving on to explore how to start making the most of the role and how to manage the day-to-day demands. From there, we will switch focus to the more long-term, strategic view of maths leadership, including how we might work with our team to develop high-quality mathematics teaching and learning for all pupils. We will then turn our attention to dealing with issues that arise in the leading of mathematics – in particular, results and accountability as well as difficult situations more generally. Following this, we will address how to go about adding to our teams, how to manage an inspection, developing improvement plans and the appraisal process, before finally touching on taking maths leadership beyond our specific school and into system leadership. Each chapter will give specific examples from my own experience and will end with a summary of the key points and advice from the chapter.

Chapter 1

Getting the job

There is an old belief in education that to get a leadership role you have to be doing the job before you start. Clearly, this doesn't sit well; if you are doing a job then you should have the title and pay commensurate with it. What I think this belief does indicate correctly is that, if you are going to apply successfully for a role in maths leadership, you will need to be able to speak from experience about how your career to date has provided the attributes, skills and knowledge necessary to be successful in the role for which you are applying. In most person specifications for maths leadership roles these boil down to (although are not limited to):

Attributes	**Skills**	**Knowledge**
• Passion for subject. • Commitment to continuing professional development of yourself and others. • Positive personal characteristics (grit, integrity, etc.).	• Excellent classroom practitioner. • Able to analyse data and plan interventions. • Able to motivate and enthuse pupils and staff. • *Able to demonstrate impact of their work.*	• Up-to-date knowledge of the latest pedagogical initiatives. • Knowledge of strategies for raising attainment. • Knowledge of wider educational landscape (may or may not be subject specific).

It won't have escaped your attention that 'demonstrating impact' has been *highlighted* here. In recent times (at least at the time of writing), Ofsted's focus on curriculum, particularly on the three I's of intent, implementation and impact, has led to a renewed focus on leaders at all levels being able to demonstrate the impact of the work they do and the initiatives, strategies and decisions they implement.[1] An important point to consider with the demonstration of impact is that it doesn't automatically lead to a reliance on numerical data. There are many ways to demonstrate the impact of an initiative depending on what we are aiming to achieve; it could be feedback from learning walks or work scrutiny, pupil voice, notes from appraisal or many other qualitative sources that demonstrate impact alongside quantitative sources of data, like attainment or progress results, behaviour points or residual measures, for example.

For all of these attributes, skills and knowledge, there are ample opportunities for a classroom teacher to demonstrate concrete experience. The key is to look for, ask for and, if necessary, manufacture opportunities to gain experience in these areas. Such opportunities might include, amongst many others:

- Starting up an enrichment club for higher attaining mathematicians.
- Leading on developing an aspect of mathematics teaching during departmental meeting/INSET time.
- Organising and helping pupils to prepare for local or national maths challenges.
- Reading research or attending conferences and implementing changes as a result (in your own practice if not across a team).
- Offering to lead on designing and implementing an intervention for lower attaining pupils.
- Analysing your own class assessment or homework data and implementing your own interventions in class.
- Negotiating an appraisal target to focus on a key area that you wish to demonstrate.

An excellent strategy to support your preparation for applying for maths leadership roles is to keep a professional journal of the opportunities you access and, importantly, the outcomes from those opportunities. For example:

- If you set up an enrichment club, how many pupils attended? Did the number of pupils attending increase? Did their results improve? Did their attitude to mathematics improve?

---

1 Ofsted, Education Inspection Framework (updated 11 July 2022). Available at: https://www.gov.uk/government/publications/education-inspection-framework/education-inspection-framework.

- If leading on developing an aspect of maths, did subsequent learning walks note improvements in the teaching and learning of this aspect? Does work scrutiny show improvements in pupils' understanding of this idea?
- If you are helping to prepare pupils for local or national maths challenges, how did they do? Was this better than in previous years?
- If you are implementing ideas from research or conferences, what did you change? What impact did the change have? Do pupils prefer the new approach? Do results show that it has benefitted pupils? Does staff voice suggest it has improved workload or well-being?
- If implementing an intervention (either across classes or within your own class), has it addressed the identified issue? Do the results show improvement? Has pupil attitude improved? Are pupils more confident in the area of the intervention?

A common issue that arises when people are applying for maths leadership roles is that they simply forget to include details of relevant experiences, either not mentioning them at all or not providing the concrete examples that can prove so crucial during the interview process. Keeping a journal of these experiences, referring to it in an application and studying it in the run-up to an interview (if needs be, printing out pages and taking them with you) are all excellent ways to ensure that you remember to mention those things that will help you to be successful in gaining the role.

Of course, the list of attributes, skills and knowledge above is not exhaustive, and every person specification is subtly different. Another important strategy to consider when you decide on a maths leadership role (or are ready to move on from one role to the next) is to look at as many person specifications and job descriptions as you can, even for roles you wouldn't necessarily consider applying for. Job descriptions can tell you a lot about what the school sees as the key aspects of the role. Are they talking about a need to develop the curriculum? Or is supporting new teachers more prominent? Is there a big emphasis on setting high expectations (which may indicate a need to support behaviour)? Or is the emphasis more on improving results?

In a lot of cases, schools have standard job descriptions that don't change from one appointment to the next, but sometimes they will tailor it to emphasise what they see as the most important priorities of the role (personally, I think more schools should do this). Even if a school is using their standard job description for a leadership role, it can still operate as an important checklist of the key responsibilities it will entail – and at the very least, it can give you some prompts to talk to others about if there are aspects you want more information about, either at your current school, the school you are interested in applying to or simply with your wider professional network.

Undoubtedly, though, the key document in any application pack is the person specification. If the job description tells you what the school expects a successful candidate to do once in post, then the person specification tells you what sort of candidate they expect to be able to fulfil those responsibilities. Looking at lots of person specifications can be really useful in highlighting any areas or experiences that you haven't yet had the opportunity to develop, and which you can then take steps to address. The first thing school leaders will usually do when shortlisting candidates (beyond noting any obvious deficiencies in qualifications or experience) will be to compare the details of the application form and covering letter (where applicable) to the essential and desirable qualities of the person specification. With a strong field, any question mark over whether a candidate has met an essential requirement of the person specification will usually lead to that candidate not being shortlisted for interview.

Interviews

When it comes to interviews there are a few common elements. Clearly, there will be an interview panel including senior staff and possibly a governor. There is usually a lesson observation, although some schools have dropped this element for senior maths leadership roles (the logic being that you wouldn't have progressed to this point without being able to teach a lesson to a good standard). There may be a pupil panel. There may be interview tasks like analysing data or observing lessons. There is often a tour of the school (don't be fooled – this is still part of the interview process and pupils and staff will feed back). How many of these and in what order will depend on the individual school.

Typically, the interview panel will focus on your vision for mathematics at the school alongside your philosophy for maths in general, and then your thinking around how you might handle certain situations. Some schools have started sending out these questions prior to interview, so candidates can prepare for them, although this practice doesn't appear to be particularly widespread. In any event, whether you see them beforehand or not, likely questions may include the following.[2]

Why do you want this maths leadership position at this school?

The important point with this question is to make sure that you tackle both why you want the position and why at that school in relatively equal measure (they may be asked as two separate questions). Your reasons for wanting the leadership role are your own, so you will have to articulate those. In terms of the school, this will depend on whether this is an internal or external promotion. If an internal promotion then, hopefully, you can talk about why you like working at the school. If an external promotion, then you must be able to talk about why the school's ethos and culture attracts you, and why you think it will fit with what you want to do in the role. Above all, though, you must ensure that you mention pupils in your answer – fundamentally, you want to make things better for pupils, and this must come across.

What is your vision for maths in this school?

The best advice here is to (a) have a vision and (b) be honest about it. This is the big question that will decide whether the future you envisage for the maths department and the one the school envisages are aligned. Assuming you have done your research on the school (and you really should), then you should be fairly confident that your visions will align. Be clear and concise, particularly about how pupils will benefit from what you want to bring into the department.

---

[2] There are other good examples of general head of department interview questions at: Engage Education, Head of Department Interview Questions (8 December 2019). Available at: https://engage-education.com/blog/head-of-department-interview-questions.

Why is maths a core subject?/ Justify the importance of maths in the school curriculum

For me, the biggest mistake here is to focus too heavily on numeracy. Of course, it is important that all pupils leave school with basic numeracy, but the ambition of mathematics education goes far beyond simple number work. The second biggest mistake is to try and invent practical relevance for topics. Yes, some careers require some parts of the school mathematics curriculum, but this is far from the norm and a poor justification for why maths gets as much, if not more, curriculum time than any other subject. There is something to be said for an answer to this question based on skills development. There are ways of thinking and problem-solving used heavily in maths that pupils won't acquire to the same depth (if at all) in their other subjects – provided, of course, that developing these skills is going to be an important part of your vision for the subject.

Personally, my favourite answer to this question centres around the exact opposite of the two poorer answers. Mathematics is fundamentally different to every other subject on the curriculum in both form and content. Learning mathematics requires pupils to engage with abstract concepts that have little to no practical relevance, at least at their level of experience, and this isn't an easy thing to do. But it is an important thing to do. Every major scientific and technological breakthrough that has happened in recent history has been pre-empted and prompted by developments in mathematics. It is these mathematical developments that provide scientists and engineers with the new language they need to push the boundaries in their own disciplines. This history, story and study of mathematics is the study of human advancement. It is also one of very few subjects in which nearly everyone can excel; all it requires is a brain, a pen and paper. All of this requires the time and prominence that maths is afforded in the curriculum.

Why should all pupils study trigonometry (or some other content)?

This is actually quite similar to the third question, in terms of the common mistake being inventing some form of pseudo-context for which trigonometry might be useful in carpentry, engineering or other real-life areas. Again, yes, there are areas beyond school where trigonometry may play a part, but this isn't a good argument for all pupils studying it. Similarly, the skills argument isn't bad (it isn't about the content; it is about the skills that pupils pick up when they learn it), but I am less happy with it on this question than I am in the previous one – is there nothing else they could study that would give them the same skills? This question asks you to justify a bit of content, so please justify the content.

What this question is really about is your curriculum thinking – where does trigonometry come from, and where does it go? Of course, it depends on the content you are asked about, but take the time to think about this content in terms of the curriculum as a whole – why is it an important step on the journey? In the case of trigonometry, it brings together important ideas around similarity and functions (if taught well) and allows pupils to deepen their understanding of these two very fundamental ideas in mathematics, and so it makes sense for all pupils to understand how trigonometry develops from these two previously studied areas.

What will be your priorities for the development of the maths department/maths teaching in this school if you are successful?

This is always a tricky question for a couple of reasons: firstly, no matter how much research you do, you can't be sure of the complete situation that the department/school is currently in and, secondly, you don't want to insult current practice.

It is fine here to qualify statements to make it clear that you will need time to understand and evaluate current practice (particularly if you are an external candidate for the role); however, you can't leave it at that. There will need to be something – either something you have picked up from your research into the school/department or something from your own convictions about mathematics and how it should be taught – that you will seek to move forward in the role for which you are applying. Key in this answer is finding a way of explaining that you want to utilise and build on strengths of current practice to help achieve your priorities; that it won't just be you doing things to your team to improve things, but it will be you working with your team and drawing on all their collective experiences and skills in order to make things better.

How would you support an underperforming teacher?

The principal point to make about addressing underperformance is the importance of securing buy-in. There needs to be a recognition that no teacher will move things forward in their practice unless they recognise that (a) there is a pressing need for it to improve, and (b) you are a person who can support that improvement, either through your own intervention or through identifying others who can help.

The start of this answer needs to be around how you ensure that the teacher recognises the need to improve, using data, pupil voice, coaching following an observation or any other strategy you have found to be successful. From there you can talk about how through training, coaching, mentoring and other support (joint planning, peer observation, etc.) you will secure the necessary improvement. At this point, unless you volunteer it (and you should), you will almost certainly be prompted to consider what actions you would take if one of these steps didn't work – that is, if you don't secure the necessary buy-in from the member of staff or you have tried some strategies and weren't getting the necessary improvement. The point of your interviewer pushing this is to ensure that you recognise that there will come a point where attempts to get buy-in have to become instructions to follow, and there will also come a point where you will need to discuss this with your senior leadership team (SLT) line manager and get further support.

How do you handle a parent who calls or emails to complain about a member of staff?

An important fact to establish here is the nature of the complaint. To do this, you should 100% be making a phone call – if the parent has called, then fine (you are already on the phone), but if the parent emails, then you should make the point that you would call back as these things are best dealt with over the phone. Once you are speaking with the parent, you will want to ascertain the particulars of the complaint – specifically, whether it is an issue of conduct or practice. An issue of conduct will need to be followed up with the member of staff (potentially involving your SLT line manager or principal if it might stray into serious misconduct or a safeguarding concern). An issue of practice will also need to be followed up but differently – it is likely to begin as a more collaborative endeavour between yourself and the member of staff to try and address whatever issue has arisen to ensure the pupil is learning again (which is, of course, the primary aim).

Pupil panels will tend to focus more on the issues that young people consider important. Questions like: 'How will you help us achieve well?', 'How do you help pupils who struggle?', 'What do you think is important for pupils studying maths?' and 'What would you do if there was a class that had a lot of disruption?' They also tend to be the place where questions that aren't to do with practice are asked, such as: 'What three words would you use to describe yourself?', 'If you weren't a teacher, what would you be?' and 'What was your favourite subject at school, and why?' In general, the point with pupil interview panels is to try not to be overly 'cool' or friendly; the best advice is to be warm and answer honestly but keep it professional.

In both interview panels, don't overlook the importance of asking your own questions. What do the pupils want from their maths department or lessons? What would they change? What do the school leadership see as the critical development areas for the maths department or maths across the school? What role does any multi-academy trust have in setting the agenda for the department or school, and how much autonomy would you have in the direction of travel? Avoid enquiring about autonomy directly – it might make you sound like a bit of a control freak when phrased this way – but asking about the role of the trust and how it supports or drives the work of the school is fine (there may well be someone from the trust on the panel).

It is particularly impressive if you can work into a question something you have picked up on throughout the day, such as: 'On my tour, a pupil told me that they do a summative test each half term. Are these tests that the department has designed or are they tests that have been bought in? How does the department or school currently use the data generated from the tests?' All interview panels will make clear that there is no need for you to ask questions, but at the same time it does reflect well if you can ask intelligent questions about the school or role to which you haven't already received answers.

School tours

You can also impress by asking questions during the tour of the school. Whether it is a group of pupils or a staff member conducting the tour, asking questions shows your interest in the school and the role, and also allows you to reveal more about yourself to those conducting the tour, which will be reported back. If pupils are leading, asking about typical experiences is always good ground: what is their typical maths lesson like? Their typical school day? Their favourite lesson? What is it like at break/lunchtime? What have they been studying in maths recently? Enquiries like this provide valuable information about how pupils view their school, and also allow you to show a warm and interested persona.

If a staff member is conducting the tour, ask about things like the curriculum model (how many hours does maths have per week/fortnight?), personal, social, health and citizenship education or form time organisation (which might be used to drive the school ethos and values), organisation of the department (do teachers typically have their own room? Is there a faculty base nearby?) and school organisation (duties, lesson timings and structure, etc.). It is also nice, where possible, to ask follow-up questions when the person conducting the tour gives some information, as it shows that you are actually listening to them (provided you aren't asking a question they have already answered).

Observed lessons

The (likely) observation of your own teaching is something that anyone applying for a maths leadership role will probably have experienced before. There are two key points to remember here. Firstly, you will almost certainly be asked to reflect on your lesson during the later panel interview, so make sure you provide yourself with opportunities to recognise details about how the lesson is going and the impact it is having. Are there any pupils who aren't clear on an aspect? What would you change in order to make sure they are?

Secondly, ensure your approach to the lesson doesn't contradict what you are planning to talk about in terms of ethos or vision for teaching maths in that department or school. If you are intending to say that you want the maths taught to be rooted in authentic, real-life problems, then make sure your lesson reflects this and shows how it can be successful. If your vision is for the department to be heavily influenced by cognitive science, then showcase how practice can include strategies like spaced retrieval, interleaved practice, goal-free problems and so on.

Although those applying for maths leadership roles will have experienced a lesson observation before, this is potentially the first time your lesson will become a reflection of what maths in your department or school would look like, so there may be problems if this doesn't match what you talk about later during the interview panel.

Data tasks

The other parts of an interview day are much more subjective. If there is a data task, then there are many forms it could take, such as looking at class-level data, year group-level data or subgroup data. However, there are a few likely commonalities:

- Make sure to focus not only on what the data suggest, but also what you would intend to do as a result of what you have identified. Is progress for the pupil premium group lower than it should be? In which case, what strategies have you seen that can help to improve their progress? Is a particular class underperforming compared to a similar class (in terms of prior attainment)? If so, how do you work with a teacher to identify the reasons for underperformance and address them? Is there an issue with a particular headline measure in the subject as a whole? If so, how would you look to drive improvement in this area across the department or school?

- Collaboration is important. When talking about the actions you might take to tackle any issues that the data appear to be highlighting, remember to bring in other voices to help. If there is an issue with pupil premium progress, include talking to a leader in charge of pupil premium strategy or provision about how to address it as part of your actions. If a class is underperforming in comparison to a parallel class, perhaps bring in the teacher of the parallel class for joint planning or include the senior leader with responsibility for teaching and learning in a discussion about how practices might be adapted for more impact. If there is underperformance across the board in relation to a key headline measure, is there another subject lead whose subject is performing better who might be able to give some advice and guidance on how they have secured these results? Showing that you recognise the importance of your work as part of a team is a crucial part of any data analysis task.

- Highlight data to which you don't have access. In most data tasks, there are figures you don't have that would be of benefit in identifying potential issues. Be sure to include details of any further data you would want to examine in order to shed more light on the situation (this may be an official question as part of the task anyway).

Lesson observations

In some cases, an interview for a maths leadership role will include an observation of a maths lesson taught by someone else; this may well be in place of a lesson that you teach. If this is a part of your day, you will generally be observing alongside someone else, either a member of the school's current leadership team or other candidates (or both). A discussion will typically follow, either round table or between yourself and the leadership team member.

In a round table discussion, it is important that you get across the points you want to make without completely dominating the discussion. In this scenario, a member of the SLT will be observing the discussion. They will be looking out for individuals who can make useful contributions whilst also respecting the opinions of others. If you persistently interrupt in order to make your own points, then it will be noted that you don't work well in collaboration. If you sit there and don't contribute to the discussion, it will be noted that either you weren't assertive enough or you didn't have any points to make. Ideally, you want to be in a position to drive the discussion without dominating and be seen to create space for others to share their thoughts and opinions, whilst also adding your own into the mix.

If the discussion is between yourself and a member of the school leadership, then it is a more straightforward situation and quite similar to the interview question about what you would want to develop in the maths department, in that you have to be careful to not be overly critical. Remember to highlight the positives and talk about how you would want those shared with others in the department, as well as being open about areas you might look to develop with the teacher and, importantly, what you would expect the impact to be. It is key in this sort of discussion that when you identify an aspect of practice that you feel could be developed, you follow up both with how you would look to develop it and why it is important that it is developed – that is, what impact you would expect the improvement to have on pupil outcomes, classroom experience and so on.

Hopefully, this advice will help you to secure that maths leadership role on which you are keen (or that you already have and you recognise some of what we have explored in your own interview experience). Once you have the role, it is time to get stuck into it.

Key points

- Audit yourself against person specifications before you start applying for maths leadership jobs, so you can identify if there are any essential criteria you still need to develop.
- Keep a professional journal of experiences and training to prompt you to talk about relevant opportunities both in an application form and during an interview.

- Be prepared to discuss your vision and ethos for mathematics teaching – and ensure any observation (of your own teaching or observing others teaching) reinforces this vision.
- Ask intelligent questions at every opportunity, but make sure they aren't questions that have already been answered either during the day or in the advert.
- Remember to include concrete examples from your own experience, and bring in demonstrated or (at least) expected impact.
- Don't forget to mention collaboration with others who can assist you in realising your vision or improving or supporting staff, such as senior leaders, other middle leaders and other teachers in your department or school.
- Everything comes back to its impact on pupil outcomes or experiences, so ensure you talk about these as much as possible.

Chapter 2

Getting stuck in

Now you have your maths leadership role, you will want to get stuck in to realise your vision. A word of warning though: don't change too much too fast. Depending on the role and the school, there might be some definite things that need to change quickly; there may be issues with outcomes or practice that need to be addressed immediately and/or there may be areas of departmental organisation that you can alter to improve the workload or well-being for your team. But change too much, too fast and this will cause anxiety and create problems for both teachers and pupils.

Quick wins

A relatively general consensus in taking on a new leadership role is to try and secure what are known as 'quick wins'. There may be a concern over the behaviour of a group of pupils or a departmental process that creates an undue amount of workload that can be dealt with immediately and give everyone a boost, whilst also illustrating to your team that you are there to support and make things better for them. Another note of caution though: quick wins that might compromise your long-term vision for mathematics in the department or school are best avoided. You also need to be wary of making any meaningful changes before you really understand the current state of play. The best piece of advice I can give you as a maths lead is to take some time to understand the true state of the department or school.

I remember my first head of department role at Oxford Spires Academy well. On my visit days prior to taking up the job, I talked to the team about what issues they would like to change. My former colleague, Jamie, mentioned that in the past the school had used a rich task-based scheme of work. At Fitzharrys, we had worked on incorporating rich tasks at the end of units of work, both as a means of assessment and to provide opportunities for pupils to apply their mathematics to more open-ended and involved problems. I therefore jumped on this and rewrote the entire Key Stage 3 schemes of work over the Christmas break to make them exclusively rich task based and then rolled them out immediately on starting the role in January, so that pupils were working in groups on tasks that were 'designed' to develop their maths through work on problems.

Whilst I am not suggesting that rich tasks are an invalid way to teach maths, there were several problems with this approach:

- I lacked the knowledge and skills to effectively design tasks and problems that could be used effectively over the course of several weeks to develop pupils' mathematical understanding beyond what they already knew.
- My team were relatively inexperienced (I and one other staff member had been teaching for around five years and the rest were either first- or second-year teachers), meaning none of us really had the knowledge or skills to make these tasks successful opportunities for pupils to develop their mathematical understanding.
- I hadn't invested any time in collaborating with others to make sure the tasks were suitable, in developing my own knowledge and skills in respect of ensuring my team could successfully implement this sort of pedagogy, or in developing the team so they could actually deliver the lessons.

The result was that we had a group of Year 7 and 8 pupils who came to maths lessons, were engaged to massively different degrees and weren't really making any progress in their mathematical understanding. This lasted until the school improvement partner came to see maths and pointed out all the issues, at which point we had to undergo yet more change to correct the hurried and ill-thought-through roll-out of the original change.

Contrast this with the implementation of the new Key Stage 3 scheme of work at Brockington that we introduced in August 2018. The scheme was in development for nearly two years before it was rolled out to pupils, and those two years were spent using all available departmental time to ensure that staff understood the aim of the scheme and how to implement it, including the particular materials (such as the different manipulatives and representations) that were crucial to its success (more on this in Chapter 4).

The clear message here is that, whilst it is tempting to get stuck in and drive change quickly, any shift needs a proportionate amount of time to be invested into it – time to collaborate and develop something sufficiently well to have the required impact, as well as ensuring that all staff have the knowledge and skills to make it successful.

So, how do you get stuck into leading maths? There are four different elements that I think are important to establish in the early days of a leadership role in maths:

1 Time together as a team is focused on teaching maths and how this happens well.
2 High standards of behaviour are expected of pupils and staff in all mathematics lessons.
3 Staff (and pupils) see you as an open leader who is interested in them and wants to hear their opinions as well as presenting your own initiatives and directives to them.
4 Getting to know your team – their strengths (both in practice and approach), areas for development and personalities.

You can work on all of these elements immediately upon taking a lead role in maths without any negative impact on the long-term vision or priorities you might already have or are beginning to develop (assuming your long-term vision isn't one where staff work in isolation, allow pupils to coast through lessons and robotically implement whatever diktats come from above without deviation). We will examine each of these factors below.

Time management

It is an unfortunate fact of school life that there are potentially a huge number of pressures that can steal attention from the core business – namely, making sure that the pupils who come through the school are well educated. There are the necessary administrative burdens, issues around class organisation (particularly in environments where pupils are set), the challenging behaviour of pupils, whole-school initiatives, data input, analysis and action – the list goes on. Crucially, though, very little of this requires the collective attention of every member of the team. Indeed, one of the key roles of the leader of maths is to manage these matters so that only the essential things actually end up at teacher level, and that only those issues that will truly benefit pupils and staff come through in a shared forum. The following strategies may prove useful.

Deal with as many of the administrative or organisational tasks as possible through email or shared documents

If you are placing an order for supplies, email out and ask staff if they would like to order anything or create a shared online order form. If you are looking at set changes, send out proposed amendments in advance of any meeting or request comments via email. Create shared data trackers so that staff can update assessment outcomes in their own time. In my latest department, there is one meeting a year, towards the end of the year, where there is some setting discussion (as there is some necessary back and forth which is better done with staff together) to ensure that we are as well organised as possible for the following year. This is always a discussion based on information sent out previously rather than starting from scratch, and it is the only occasion when any time together as a department isn't spent working on developing practice.

Anything done collectively with data needs to be about action, not analysis

When it comes to data input, ask staff to complete it individually and then check it prior to a meeting so you are happy. There is something to say for having time when staff are able to talk about what their data shows. However, the point of this discussion should be around the actions they are going to take as a result. This will allow others in the team to learn from and challenge those actions. This requires staff to have engaged with their data prior to any meeting, and still allows you and the team to see the results of what their analysis has highlighted.

Tackle behaviour issues individually

I remember attending meetings (which I wasn't running) where time was set aside for members of staff to bring up behaviour concerns about pupils or classes. I am sure you can imagine that this section of the meeting always ended up dominating the proceedings and meant that anything else on the agenda was squashed in terms of both time and importance. I don't blame either the head of department or the staff for this; put a group of teachers together and ask them to talk about concerns around behaviour and, no matter what school you are in, there will be things to talk about.

Indeed, there is something very cathartic about being able to have a good old moan about a pupil or class who are causing you issues, but this is generally a waste of the rest of the team's time. These matters can be tackled, at least initially, with the member of staff individually (we will look at strategies for how to support staff with poor pupil behaviour in the next chapter). There may come a point when you want to involve other members of the team, but airing all of this in an open forum isn't a particularly good use of everyone's time.

> In general, creation should be done separately (at worst in very small groups), whilst critiquing and perfecting are better done collectively

This point is aimed at whole-school initiatives but applies equally to departmental developments as well. Collective creation is a very tricky thing to pull off; having a lot of voices trying to steer the initial development of a resource, programme or project often means that progress is significantly slower and doesn't usually lead to higher quality. Generally, a better approach is to create something (or task each team member to create something individually) and then use the team time to discuss and improve what has been created.

> What is being shared isn't as important as the act of sharing

If your team isn't used to sharing practice in an open forum, then developing a culture of sharing will serve your purposes well down the line, even if the practice doesn't always fit with what you want to aim for in the longer term. Instead, see this as a way of helping you to gain an insight into the current practice of your team and to establish the good practice of sharing; the content of what is communicated can evolve over time.

Balance what you do yourself with what the team contributes

I am not referring to continuing professional development (CPD) or curriculum development here, although there is also a balance to be found in these areas. I mean matters like policy or procedure writing, improvement plans and so on. It is very tempting to take on a lot (if not all) of these sorts of pressures in order to protect your team's time. However, this can lead to you spending all your time on administration and not engaging with the business of actually driving things forward in the teaching of maths. The bulk of this type of work will (rightly) fall to you, but there will be situations where the choice is between each member of the team doing 10 minutes of work and you doing an hour. There are also some tasks that it will be of real benefit for other members of the team to do or get involved with (we will look at delegation and distributing leadership in Chapter 5).

Behaviour and practice

If you are lucky, you will be in a school where high standards of behaviour and practice are already well embedded. In many schools, they are more variable; even where behaviour and practice are generally good, there may well be pockets of poorer behaviour or practice. This is definitely something that you should start dealing with early on in your tenure as maths lead, even if they aren't matters that can be fixed quickly.

Of course, the extent to which you are responsible for supporting teachers with behaviour will depend on the specifics of your role. In primary schools this will generally be the province of the SLT rather than the subject leads, whereas in the secondary or tertiary sector the head of subject often has a direct role in supporting their departmental staff with managing behaviour.

We will explore in more detail some strategies for supporting staff with behaviour management in Chapter 3 and supporting underperforming staff in Chapter 5. However, when it comes to setting high standards there are some key messages and strategies that are worth starting with at the outset.

Considered seating plans are a must for all classes

As well as being a vehicle to ensure that staff are considering the dynamics of their classroom, seating plans send a clear message to pupils about where the authority in the classroom lies. When I design a seating plan, I always make it clear that my goal is to make sure the environment is one in which they can learn well. To that end, if pupils feel the seating plan isn't meeting that goal, they are welcome to discuss this with me at a time when we are both free. However, I won't allow changes at the beginning of a lesson (the old, 'So and so isn't here today, can I sit in their seat?'). This is also what I encourage my staff to do, and on rare occasions I will mandate this if I feel it is necessary.

Introduce pupils to how maths lessons are run

In my most recent director of maths role at Brockington, we have developed a relatively standard structure for our Key Stage 3 lessons as part of our recent scheme of work developments. The first lesson that all staff complete with Year 7 classes introduces them to the core structures of a maths lesson – what to do when they come into the classroom, how example-problem pairs work, how to respond to diagnostic multiple-choice questions and so on. Whether or not there is a typical format for lessons, pupils need to be taught how to interact with different classroom activities – when to have pens down and be listening, when to be working individually and when to be working collaboratively (and how to work collaboratively).

In addition, pupils need to be taught why these aspects of a lesson are important – why they need to practise skills even if they feel they can do them, why they need to discuss different prompts or collaborate on different activities, and how these will help them to learn mathematics. Each teacher can do this individually with their classes as suits them and their approach (where there isn't a standard approach), which has the added benefit of teachers having to consider elements of their routine practice and how they help pupils.

Consistent application of rewards and sanctions

To be clear, when I talk about consistency in this context, I am not necessarily talking department or school-wide but rather consistency within a class. One of the most common complaints from pupils who repeatedly find themselves on the wrong side of sanctions is that they are 'picked on'. Now, a considerable amount of this is due to their own behaviour. However, it is much easier to challenge this perception if it is demonstrable that a teacher is ruthlessly consistent in their application of sanctions, and so a pupil's attention can be redirected into clear systems by which they can earn rewards.

Parental contact is crucial for both positives and issues

Parental contact has consistently been found to support pupils whose behaviour is impacting on their own or their peers' learning.[1] In my experience, and that of others, the use of home contact as a 'reward' for high-quality work or effort is also a key strategy for encouraging a positive learning environment.[2] It is easy for a team to forgo parental contact when there are time pressures in other areas, so helping to create the space for this to happen and reminding staff of its importance are excellent ways to help create high standards across a team.

Share good practice that you see

One of the things you will certainly do as a maths leader is to go and see your team doing their work in the maths classroom. An excellent strategy when you are conducting learning walks (or whatever term is used in your setting) is to highlight and then share the good practice you see. This can be anything from sending a team email, to

---

1 Ofsted and A. Spielman, HMCI Commentary: Managing Behaviour Research (12 September 2019). Available at: https://www.gov.uk/government/speeches/research-commentary-managing-behaviour.
2 E. Aguilar, The Power of the Positive Phone Call Home, *Edutopia* (20 August 2012; updated 7 August 2015). Available at: https://www.edutopia.org/blog/power-positive-phone-call-home-elena-aguilar.

updating a shared document pinpointing the examples of excellent practice you have witnessed, to asking people to speak briefly about their approach to teaching a particular bit of maths or an effective strategy they are using in a departmental meeting. This will start to communicate to your team what high standards in practice look like, as well as drawing attention to yourself and the team of any staff members who are notable by their absence when it comes to finding examples of quality teaching.

Leadership style

One of the best ways to secure buy-in with a new team is to listen to them and act on what they say. As well as encouraging teacher agency (which research shows is important for job satisfaction and retention[3]), it also gives you a bank of goodwill so that, when you do need to act unilaterally, your team are more inclined to go with you. This sort of leadership leans towards the affiliative and democratic leadership styles, which are two of six identified leadership styles that are effective in different scenarios.[4] In reality, a leader will move through all of these styles at different times, depending on the situation. In doing so, it will be important to reflect on the following points.

Consider how committed you are to a certain action or approach

There will be times when you want a definite outcome and opt to take a specific approach to achieve it. There will be other times when you want a definite outcome but you aren't committed to a particular approach to make it happen. It is these latter situations that you want to open up to your team for their input: present the problem you want to solve or the result you want to achieve and ask for suggestions on how to go about tackling it, before reaching a consensus on the way forward.

---

3 J. Worth and J. Van den Brande, *Teacher Autonomy: How Does It Relate to Job Satisfaction and Retention?* (Slough: National Foundation for Educational Research, 2020). Available at: https://www.nfer.ac.uk/teacher-autonomy-how-does-it-relate-to-job-satisfaction-and-retention.
4 The other four are coercive, authoritative, pacesetting and coaching – see American University School of Education, Six Highly Effective Education Leadership Styles [blog] (12 July 2019). Available at: https://soeonline.american.edu/blog/education-leadership-styles.

Providing you don't dictate the outcome or the approach too often, this sort of collaborative leadership approach will make it much more likely that your team will respond positively to you as a leader. The one exception to this is when you have a very inexperienced team; in this case, you might act more coercively or authoritatively more often as your team will be looking to you for leadership on action as well as outcome.

Allow people to act on their own initiative

One of the biggest mistakes I used to make as a leader of maths is to take people's ideas from them and action them myself. A member of my team would make a suggestion and my response would be, 'Good idea, I'll get right on that.' One of the most powerful shifts I made in leading maths was to change this response to, 'Good idea, can you look into that and let me know what you need?' Not only does this help to reduce your own workload, but it gives your team a way of contributing beyond their teaching, which is good for their own development and their sense of worth (particularly when you remember to praise and thank them later and highlight their contribution to the team).

Talk to pupils!

This applies in all situations. Pupil having trouble in maths class? Talk to them. Pupil making poor behavioural choices? Talk to them. Conduct regular pupil voice sessions around the subject in general and potentially around the implementation and impact of initiatives you introduce. Don't get me wrong: there will be times when you have to lay down the law with a pupil, regardless of what they might have to say on a subject, and there are times when you won't be able to take pupils' opinions into account (young people are notorious for wanting things that aren't the best for them[5]). However, as long as you explain this to them and why you have chosen a different approach, most will accept it.

---

5 See, for example, N. Kornell and R. A. Bjork, Learning Concepts and Categories: Is Spacing the 'Enemy of Induction'?, *Psychological Science*, 19(6) (2008), 585–592. https://doi.org/10.1111%2Fj.1467-9280.2008.02127.x

Visit staff just to hear about their day

When I led the maths team at Brockington, I would try to pop into different teachers' classrooms at the end of the day as often as possible, just to talk about how their day had gone. In fact, this is something I haven't done as much since taking the role of assistant principal, due to the heads of subject I line-manage being spread throughout the school, but I am going to try and do more of it in the future.

I always found that an informal chat with two or three members of the team highlighted issues that I wouldn't have been aware of otherwise, such as concerns about a pupil or class, and also made the staff feel that I was genuinely interested in them. The important point is that it was never about me going in to try and solve a problem or ask them to do a job, it was just to have a conversation, wherever it led. I would typically start simply with, 'How was your day?' and let the talk flow where it wanted to go.

Where possible, have an open subject base rather than a single office

I suspect that this topic will apply to secondary schools more than primary schools (depending on the exact structure and make-up of the school), but I always found a central team space invaluable in having conversations throughout the day. We are lucky at Brockington that, after my first year there, we moved to a corridor that had what we call a 'knuckle room' – a large room (although smaller than a classroom) on the corner between two classrooms – in which we have set up several workspaces (as well as being able to house small-group interventions). At Oxford Spires Academy, I turned one of the maths classrooms into a department base (which would occasionally house A level maths classes when no other rooms were available).

Some might think that it is less than ideal to have pupils being taught in staff workspaces, but I have found that it can actually spark interesting conversations and involvement from other staff. With virtually all confidential information now stored online, rather than in paper files, the concerns about pupils seeing things they shouldn't are much reduced compared to the beginning of my career. For me, the benefits far outweigh the occasional need to move back into a private classroom or office to access something you can't risk others seeing.

Getting to know your team

Although you can plan to introduce certain practices, approaches or ways of working when new to a maths leadership role, you will find it difficult to plan the effective implementation of these until you have a good grasp of the strengths and weaknesses of your team. This goes for everything from their subject knowledge and pedagogy, right through to their personal attributes, like how well they work with other staff members or how they respond to different types of task.

We will explore how to utilise the team for different types of work in Chapters 4 and 5, where we look at strategic leadership and development, but a good place to start getting stuck in is learning about your team and their skills.

Visit lessons as often as you can

The purpose of lessons visits is two-fold. Firstly, they will allow you to get a sense of what the prevailing pedagogies are and to pick up on potential strengths and weaknesses in subject knowledge or subject-specific pedagogy. There is no point planning to expand the use of mini whiteboards if your team isn't consistently good at designing and asking the sorts of questions that allow for the quick identification of misconceptions. You can't introduce a consistent method for a particular aspect of the curriculum if not all of your staff have the subject knowledge to explain it well. Getting a strong understanding of the baseline when it comes to subject and pedagogical knowledge is fundamental to being able to implement changes.

Secondly, you will gain an insight into the different ways your team respond to lesson visits. Who gets flustered every time you walk into the room? Who is regularly having to firefight around the classroom because the pupils don't understand the whole-class instruction? Are there people who become more combative if they feel under scrutiny? Who plays up to the audience?

Obviously, you will need to make it clear that you aren't there to judge; try to put staff at ease with the idea that you are just trying to get a sense of what is happening across the team with regard to teaching and practice. This is one of those issues that can benefit from discussion with the team beforehand, and potentially even agreeing some elements of the process with them (how often, how long, what actions follow, etc.), but it is definitely something that needs to happen early in your tenure.

Pay attention to the dynamics in team meetings

The way your team works together when they are collectively discussing or working on practice tells you a lot about them individually. Who is always offering opinions? Who is often criticising but suggesting little constructively? Who is just sitting there disengaged unless interacted with directly? How do they respond when that interaction happens? Which team members will happily get involved in small group planning activities or discussions? Who volunteers to feed back from the group? Who is clearly ambitious and wants to be noticed? All of these little insights will serve you well down the line when you are looking to get colleagues involved in developing new practices across the team.

Consider auditing subject knowledge and pedagogy

Finding out about your team's subject knowledge doesn't have to mean everyone doing a SATs/GCSE/A level exam paper to see what maths they can do (although I remember having to do this when I started my PGCE). A knowledge audit can be conducted in numerous ways, some more subtle and some more overt. You might audit subject knowledge and pedagogy across several weeks' worth of meetings by bringing along some interesting questions or prompts (or sending them out beforehand) and asking the team to talk about how they would explain the maths underlying them, or asking for the team collectively to come up with as many different approaches as they can (whilst being very aware of who is offering what). If you are sending the questions out beforehand, don't make it too far in advance – a day or two is enough for people to consider their approaches. More than this, and they are likely either to forget or to discuss it at length prior to the meeting. This approach has the added bonus that it serves as a development activity as well as an auditing activity.

Alternatively, you might be more direct and ask each member of the team to RAG (red, amber, green) rate their perception of how well they know and can teach different elements of the curriculum. You need to keep in mind that this is only their perception, but this knowledge can be as powerful as asking them to answer actual maths questions because, as a leader, we often deal with perception as much as (if not more than) we deal with objective reality (if such a thing exists).

Talk to your leadership team

If you are in a new setting and working with an unfamiliar team, then it is well worth having a conversation with your SLT line manager and other members of the leadership team about your team. The person in charge of teaching and learning may have valuable information about any strengths or issues that have been recognised in the pedagogy of different staff members. Whoever line managed your predecessor (which may well be your current line manager) may have an insight into the approaches they used to help manage the team or any difficulties they experienced. Your predecessor may even still be at the current setting if they were promoted (or took a different role), so you can consult with them about their view of the team. Talking to your team's peers about them can be tricky – it can be seen as asking people to report on their colleagues, but talking to other leaders should be fine.

Arrange or join in social events

Social events allow you to see your team in a different light. Whether it is birthday celebrations, team meals or wider school social events, they are a real chance to find out more about what makes your team members tick. It also allows you to see who doesn't attend these events. To be clear, it isn't a negative if a staff member doesn't attend social events, but it does tell you something. Do they have a very hectic home life? Are they uncomfortable in larger social situations?

This sort of information can be very useful when it comes to planning development opportunities or asking staff to contribute to a piece of departmental work.

Having got stuck into the role of maths leader, things will quickly start to settle down into some kind of routine. We will now turn our attention to the day-to-day management of your team, which is an important part of the job.

Key points

- Don't change too much too fast – and make sure you invest the appropriate amount of time beforehand to make the change successful.
- Go for quick wins, but only if they don't compromise your long-term vision.
- Make sure time together as a team is spent developing maths teaching.
- Prioritise high standards of both pupil and staff work.
- Establish yourself as an open and democratic leader.
- Get to know your team, both in terms of their subject knowledge/pedagogy and personality/character.

Chapter 3

Day-to-day management

A big part of leading maths is the daily management of learning across the department or school. This includes responsibilities like supporting teachers with the behaviour of pupils or classes, potentially helping to set up cover work for absent staff, monitoring teaching practice and dealing with admin.

Managing behaviour

When it comes to supporting teachers with behaviour, the overriding message is that individuals need to be empowered to tackle issues independently wherever possible. This can include reviewing seating plans alongside the teacher and suggesting changes that the teacher then implements, or observing lessons and discussing strategies that the teacher then employs in lessons; the list goes on.

Several books have been written about how teachers can manage behaviour, and it isn't my intent to rewrite all of their advice here (particularly as different people recommend very different approaches).[1] However, there may well come a point where you need to intervene more directly with pupils or classes. I have found the following approaches to be useful.

RAG rating the behaviour of pupils in a class

Occasionally, teachers will feel that a whole class has gone completely off the rails and will be unsure how to bring the atmosphere back to a purposeful one where the pupils are learning. Even in this

---

1   See, for example, P. Dix, *When the Adults Change, Everything Changes: Seismic Shifts in School Behaviour* (Carmarthen: Independent Thinking Press, 2017); and M. Finnis, *Independent Thinking on Restorative Practice: Building Relationships, Improving Behaviour and Creating Stronger Communities* (Carmarthen: Independent Thinking Press, 2021).

situation, it is rarely the entire class that is causing the issue. In the past, I have asked teachers to go down the class register and RAG rate each pupil as follows:

- Red: This pupil actively makes it more difficult for teaching and learning to take place.
- Amber: This pupil will join in with disruptive behaviour but rarely instigates it.
- Green: This pupil generally attempts to continue learning despite the disruption being caused by others.

I will then meet with each of the pupils and let them know the following:

- Red: They are causing issues in the class, which is stopping teaching and learning from taking place, and I am going to be involved in getting them back on track. Normally, this involves contacting home and/or placing the pupil on subject report.
- Amber: They need to stop involving themselves in other pupils' disruptive behaviour, and if they continue they will be subject to the same approaches I am taking with the 'red' pupils. (For clarity, I don't call them the red pupils; I just state the approaches – for example, 'If you are still causing concern in two weeks, I will be placing you on subject report.')
- Green: It has been recognised that the atmosphere in the class isn't ideal, but it has also been recognised that they are trying to make the best of it. I thank them for not getting involved in the disruptive behaviour of others, which I will be tackling.

Holding a parent/carer meeting with the teacher also present

The key point I try to keep in mind whenever I meet with parents or carers is that they and I want the same thing – namely, for their child to be happy and successful in class. A good way to approach these meetings is to look to make negotiated changes on the part of both the teacher and the pupil. For example, if we need the pupil to stay in their seat, as they have a habit of getting up and walking about to chat to others, then we may negotiate a seat move to help the pupil comply with the request. Whatever behaviour we want the pupil to change, we will look to negotiate something that the pupil or parent might suggest would help them to comply.

The purpose of this is two-fold. Firstly, it shows the pupil and parent that we are trying to work together to solve problems for the pupil. Secondly, it means that the pupil has little recourse if they don't change their behaviour; we have provided the support they and their parents said was required but their behaviour hasn't improved. This then strengthens the argument for further actions that might be needed to tackle the pupil's behaviour.

Changing class memberships or teachers

This is typically a last-resort scenario, but in the past I have had to swap teachers around when a relationship between a teacher and a class is irrevocably damaged. When doing this, I generally swap the teacher out of the year group altogether – for example, I might pick up a teacher's class in Year 9 and ask them to take on my Year 8 class. Alternatively, I have made wholesale changes to two parallel classes – for example, in one case I created a group entirely of boys and a parallel group entirely of girls. This isn't something I would recommend, as it ultimately removes the teacher from the situation (which feels like admitting defeat). However, we must keep in mind that the number one responsibility is to ensure that the pupils are learning, and if other options have been exhausted then this sort of change must at least be considered.

Covering absences

Staff will occasionally miss work. This may be due to a planned absence for a meeting or to attend professional development, or unplanned through illness or a family emergency. In many cases, staff will set cover work themselves (although they may still need support in ensuring the work is available for the pupils) but, particularly in the case of unplanned absence, it may be that the teacher is unable to set appropriate cover work.

In primary schools, the person responsible for this will vary: it may be another teacher of the same year group (where one exists), a phase leader or a member of school leadership, although it might be that a subject leader is involved in setting the cover for their subject. In secondary schools, this is generally handled by the head of department. In both settings, the challenge is ensuring the high-quality continuation of the curriculum whilst the class is working with a cover teacher, unqualified teacher or higher level teaching assistant.

In mathematics, we are quite lucky in that there are several video resources that effectively explain isolated parts of a concept or process. Websites such as Corbett Maths,[2] the Oak National Academy,[3] Seneca Learning[4] or even YouTube[5] (as well as other paid-for sites) can provide supplementary instruction in the absence of the usual class teacher. Of course, what these may not do is approach the concept or process in the way you would ideally want it approached as part of a well-sequenced curriculum. In this case, it may simply be better to set tasks that allow the pupils to practise working with previously taught concepts or processes. Some schools or departments may have a bank of these tasks available automatically for organising this.

In order to set tasks based on previously taught content, the subject leader must have a reasonable idea of where classes are in the curriculum or be able to acquire this knowledge quickly. This can be achieved by ensuring that pupil books are easily accessible, so that a quick check of a few books will tell you what the pupils in a class have been studying recently; by having an electronic tracker that staff must fill out when a unit has been completed (this can be tied to unit assessment, which we will cover in Chapter 4); or by having a lesson-by-lesson tracker where teachers are following a more pre-scribed curriculum. For example, the White Rose curriculum is broken down into individual steps within each unit, so it is possible to track which step classes are on as well as use the resources tied to this curriculum as part of setting cover work.[6]

In addition to pinpointing where classes are in the curriculum, a subject leader will also need to know (if they are going to be involved in setting cover work) when teachers are actually absent. In the case of planned absence, I would expect staff to inform me well in advance of the absence, and I would try and catch up with them the day before to ensure that all the cover work was in place

---

2 See https://corbettmaths.com.
3 See https://www.thenational.academy.
4 See https://senecalearning.com/en-GB.
5 See https://www.youtube.com.
6 See https://whiterosemaths.com/resources?year=year-1-new.

and appropriate. In the case of unplanned absence, I would expect staff to message me on the morning of the absence (alongside whichever member of the school staff was responsible for deploying cover). This would allow me to ensure that I was in school early enough to organise the necessary cover work. If this didn't happen, I would make sure to follow up with the staff member on their return and reiterate the expectations around absence.

All of this guidance assumes that the absence will be relatively short, maybe only a day or two. In the case of a long-term absence, then clearly setting practice tasks isn't going to be sufficient; pupils will need to continue to progress through the curriculum. If you are lucky, then it may be that you can appoint a supply/cover teacher who has the skills and experience to plan for that progress. However, it is just as likely that you will get a cover teacher who will only teach the lessons they are given. In this case, a leader needs a long-term plan for how to ensure the best possible provision for the class or classes that will be covered, which might include the following.

Asking a teacher of a parallel or similar ability class to share their planning

Inviting another teacher to share their lesson planning would be quite typical in a primary setting, but it works equally well in a secondary environment. Rather than taking on lots of extra planning as the subject lead, this can be shared out amongst the team. In schools where classes are set by attainment or ability, this might include asking the teacher of a parallel set (if one exists) or a set at a similar level to provide what they are planning for their own class to the cover teacher. If teaching mixed-attainment/ability pupils, then it might simply be sharing out planning across several members of the team. Provided no one is unduly burdened compared to their colleagues, then a good team will normally be happy to offer support in this way.

Redistributing teachers across the classes

Reallocating teachers would generally be more applicable in the secondary sector. What might be worth considering in the event of long-term absence is to redeploy your team to teach some of the cover lessons and use the supply/cover teacher to teach some of your team's lessons, particularly where classes are scheduled to sit assessments or other activities requiring minimal teacher input. This means that lots of classes get a little bit of cover, which may be better than a few classes getting lots of cover. Of course, this could also be applied to primary schools, where teachers could be redistributed from parallel or other year groups on a rotational basis for a day or part of a day – again, particularly where this corresponds with lessons that might require less teacher input or expertise.

Collapsing classes

The collapsing of classes is also best suited to the secondary sector, where it is often the case that multiple classes are being taught maths at the same time (for example, in my current school, half of each year group from Year 8 upwards are being taught concurrently). One strategy I have used in the past to cope with long-term absence is to collapse classes together, using the cover/supply teacher to work as a classroom assistant. This has included two small classes (numbering under 15 pupils) being combined into one larger class, and two larger classes (nearly 30 pupils each) being relocated into a larger space and taught together. There have also been occasions where lessons have been streamed live into the classroom next door, and the teacher and the supply teacher have switched back and forth between classes to supervise and offer support.

Monitoring

One of the biggest mistakes that middle (and senior) leaders often make when it comes to monitoring teaching practice is to try and force the same process to work as a development activity for teachers. The problem is that the two goals are incompatible. The purpose of monitoring is to make sure that the pupils' experience meets an acceptable standard as defined by the department, school or Department for Education. Monitoring is best done frequently and with a relatively light touch, which is why processes like short lesson visits and book looks have replaced full lesson observations over the years.

This doesn't mean that the results of lesson visits or book looks can't be shared with the team. It is always worth highlighting the good practice you come across whilst monitoring, so the rest of team can discuss and learn from it. However, this isn't the same as a structured programme of development that supports both individuals and the team collectively to move their practice forward. We will look more at planning professional development in Chapters 5 and 11, but when it comes to monitoring, the key point is to make it about the team, not the individual.

A big issue with observation for monitoring, rather than agreed development areas, is the temptation for teachers to put on a show, whether this is planning or responding differently in the classroom or suddenly marking all of their books (I have known staff to do this even when book marking wasn't required!). To try and mitigate against this reaction, we can impress upon the team that monitoring isn't attributed to the individual – in particular, it doesn't form part of performance management or any other record attributed to the teacher.

This doesn't mean that we shouldn't directly address any significant concerns with practice that we encounter whilst monitoring, but we should also bear in mind that we may not be seeing typical practice in a single monitoring session. What we can identify, though, are patterns of practice across the team that might need to be improved: are pupils remembering what they are being taught? Are there enough opportunities for pupils to practise applying key techniques? Are pupils completing the work that would be expected of them? Where improvements do need to be made, even if not the case in every single classroom, we bring them back to the team to tackle collectively so that everyone's expertise can be utilised.

Admin

The role of maths lead will inevitably include some administration. There will be action and improvement plans to write, data analysis to complete, potentially a budget to manage, all sorts of email requests and meetings to attend, and more besides. These tasks vary greatly from school to school, so the best advice if you are new to the school is to talk this through with your senior leader link or other middle leaders to get their advice on what is expected. (We will look in more detail at dealing with results in Chapter 6 and subject improvement plans in Chapter 10.)

What all of these responsibilities will impact on is your time, so we will finish this chapter with some time management tips.

Set your boundaries

There is no escaping the fact that taking a leadership role will impinge on your time. You will need to accept this and plan for it. The first things to fix are your own non-negotiables. If you go to a gym class at 6pm every Wednesday, then make sure that time is set aside. If Saturday afternoon is your time for socialising with friends, then block it out. If Sunday lunch with the family is a fixture, then reserve that time. Once these engagements are decided, then look at the times you are prepared to stretch into. Are you happy to do an hour or two in the evening after your evening meal? Or do you prefer to stay an extra hour at school to get things finished before you leave? Personally, I always find it difficult to work once I get home, so I will happily work from 8am to 6pm (or occasionally later when needed) if it means I don't have to work too often in the evening or at the weekend (although I will sometimes do some work on Sunday evening just to get things sorted for the week). You must find the times that work for you and try and stick to them, including the times when you absolutely cannot be working.

Make the best use of any time you are given

The role of maths subject lead at secondary or tertiary level will generally come with a reduced teaching timetable, ostensibly due to the fact that they will have line management responsibility for their departmental staff. A primary school maths lead is much less likely to be given extra non-contact time outside of their normal preparation, planning and assessment allowance. Either way around, the time you have during the school day must be utilised effectively. Of utmost importance is to plan what you want to accomplish in that time, although this doesn't always mean that you will get those tasks done! Sometimes other things will get in the way or the task takes longer than you first thought, but it is very easy to fritter away time if you don't have a clear idea about how you intend to use it.

This includes taking time to relax; sometimes we need time in the day to slow down even if it means having to do more later. I mentioned in Chapter 2 the importance of a subject base. It isn't unusual to find us playing cards or darts in the base, particularly when we have 'gained time' once the Year 11 exams are over. I have even seen the central table in the base turned into a table tennis table with the creative use of some spare box files to act as a net! I trust my team to get the important things done, so if they (and I) need a bit of time in the day to de-stress and socialise in order to be more productive later on, then so be it.

Keep the Pareto principle in mind

Broadly speaking, the Pareto principle suggests (at least in the context of teaching or leading) that 20% of the jobs we do or the time we spend will cause 80% of the effective output we create.[7] What this really means is that, whilst it might be tempting to keep working on something until it is as polished as it can possibly be, that extra time isn't likely to be repaid in extra effectiveness. The role of subject lead is no place for perfectionism; every leader must learn to get to a point where they say, 'That will do.'

For me, that 20% was always about support for my team, either background support systems (like resources or medium-term plans) or on-the-ground support systems (like helping with behaviour or organising departmental meetings). This meant that things like data analysis got less attention. Yes, I would identify key pupils,

---

[7] For those who haven't come across the Pareto principle before, Olivia Guy Evans provides some useful information: O. Guy Evans, Pareto Principle (The 80-20 Rule): Examples & More, *Simply Psychology* (9 February 2023). Available at: https://www.simplypsychology.org/pareto-principle.html.

subgroups and so on, but I wouldn't keep going and going to the *n*th degree, breaking down subgroups into subgroups until every possible combination of pupil characteristics had been considered like some gigantic multi-circle Venn diagram. I knew this would take an awful lot of time, and it wouldn't produce the increase in outcomes over the simpler analysis to make it worthwhile.

Day-to-day management is a significant part of the role of a subject leader, and for some it is the reason they take on the role – to be that supportive daily presence around their team. Personally though, and for many others I know, the drive to lead maths lay in the strategic power of the role – the ability to shape the long-term direction of how maths is taught across their school in order to try and improve things for as many pupils as possible. It is this strategic leadership that we will explore in Chapter 4.

Key points

- When teachers require support with the behaviour of pupils or classes, try to help them handle it themselves before you step in – and keep them involved at all times, even when you do have to step in.
- If you are setting cover work, consider what you want it to achieve and make sure there are processes in place to make this as easy as possible.
- If there is a need for long-term cover, consider how this can be delegated or classes reorganised so you aren't massively overburdened.
- Monitoring standards and developing teachers are rarely possible through the same process. If the focus of an activity is monitoring, then concentrate on doing that.
- Monitoring is about the standards of the team, not the individual (unless there are significant concerns with an individual).
- The biggest issue in managing the admin burden of leadership is organising your own time, so you can work as effectively as possible. Don't waste time chasing perfection that won't have a significant impact on performance.

Chapter 4
Strategic leadership

As maths lead, one of your major responsibilities is to decide and implement the long-term strategic direction of the subject. This may include organising the curriculum, deciding how (and potentially when) pupils are assessed, the links that the maths curriculum has with other subjects and possibly setting up subject policy and procedures.

Curriculum planning

Curriculum planning is a complex process for any subject, but it is particularly so with school-level mathematics. Whereas in some subjects the order of content (or, indeed, the actual content itself) is less important in allowing pupils to make sense of the subject matter, the order of content in maths is crucial. There are simply some ideas in mathematics that you cannot make sense of unless you have understood prerequisite ideas.

However, it isn't as simple as figuring out the correct order of ideas and then teaching them one after the other because mathematical ideas tend to come together and build on one another. Take addition and multiplication, for example. Addition is clearly a prerequisite for multiplication, as one of the first models for multiplication that pupils learn about is repeated addition. However, another model for multiplication is unitising (e.g. 4×5 can be seen as four things worth 5 or five things worth 4) and unitising can be used to explain certain properties of addition (e.g. it can help pupils to see why $5.2 \times 7 + 5.2 \times 3 = 5.2 \times 10$ as having seven things worth 5.2 and three things worth 5.2 giving 10 things worth 5.2). What this means is that very careful consideration needs to be given to which aspects of different mathematical ideas are going to be explored when these concepts appear in the curriculum.

The situation is further complicated by the fact that all pupils, no matter what stage of education they are in, will already have different knowledge of these concepts. A good curriculum needs to meet all pupils where they are, providing them with a path to progress from their pre-existing understanding to the point where we want them to be by the time they leave us. However, this doesn't mean that all pupils need to start their maths curriculum with different concepts – that is, we don't need some pupils in a class studying addition whilst others are studying multiplication. Indeed, this often leads to teachers having to try and manage too many different curricula to be effective in any of them.

So, how do we build an effective maths curriculum? I don't think anyone has completely answered this question, but the following points definitely need to be considered.

Learn from the work of others

Whilst the search for the 'perfect' maths curriculum continues (and may not even exist), several curricula have been designed for school-level maths. The White Rose Maths curriculum,[1] the Mathematics Enhancement Programme[2] and the Complete Mathematics curriculum[3] are all widely utilised across the UK and can be used either directly or as a start point for a more bespoke curriculum.

In addition to specific maths curricula, engaging in research and writing around curriculum design in general is also worthwhile. One of the top writers in this area is Mary Myatt, who has written a number of books on the subject.[4]

Ensure time is given to establishing and practising key ideas

However you decide to construct the curriculum, if it is going to be effective in ensuring that pupils learn the required concepts, then enough time has to be given to each of those concepts, both in terms

---

1 See https://whiterosemaths.com.
2 See https://www.cimt.org.uk/projects/mep/index.htm.
3 See https://completemaths.com/classroom.
4 See https://www.marymyatt.com/books.

of the initial teaching of the idea and to work with the idea and become comfortable with it. If this means that some pupils are working on ideas they are already relatively secure on, then so be it.

There was a time in the early 2000s when it was felt that pupils had to be moved on to more challenging work or concepts as soon as they had shown even the barest fluency in the current idea. Thankfully, this notion is now slowly drifting away. The analogy I always use is professional footballers doing passing drills in training. They don't do these drills because they can't pass – they are some of the best passers in the world; they do the drills because they want to continue to be some of the best passers in the world!

Plan for the interleaving and interweaving of content

In recent years, there has been a great deal of study into how to structure learning so that it is most effective. One of the ideas that has come to the fore is the efficacy of interleaving content. Broadly speaking, this means providing opportunities for pupils to practise previously learned material in conjunction with material they are currently studying.[5]

Alongside this are opportunities for interweaving, which means combining mathematical ideas within a single task – for example, when pupils are finding perimeters of shapes, including shapes that have fractional, decimal or surd lengths, they have to practise adding these types of numbers alongside the calculation of perimeter.[6]

One of the big positives of both interleaving and interweaving is that they allow teachers to check whether pupils have retained their understanding of previously taught ideas over time and, if necessary, highlight the need for the reteaching of concepts.

---

5 The Learning Scientists have produced a podcast giving more detail: Learning Scientists, Episode 8: Interleaving (6 December 2017). Available at: https://www.learningscientists.org/learning-scientists-podcast/2017/12/6/episode-8-interleaving.
6 The Interwoven Maths website has more information and lots of tasks that exemplify the idea: https://interwovenmaths.com.

Involve your team

Unless you are going to be the only person teaching mathematics in your school, you will be relying on your team to deliver the curriculum. This means involving them at every stage of the design process, even (as I alluded to in Chapter 2) if it is only to discuss and adapt something you have designed or sourced. This will include the overall programme of study, the sequencing, the resources and the materials – everything that goes into your curriculum.

If they are going to be responsible for delivering the outcomes you desire, your team will need to understand what your curriculum is trying to achieve and the key elements within it that will help them to achieve that aim.

Take your time

As I also alluded to in Chapter 2, curriculum design (or redesign) and implementation should be a slow process. Practices don't change overnight! When we redesigned the Key Stage 3 curriculum at Brockington, I knew I wanted to focus on increasing pupils' understanding of mathematical ideas, rather than just learning how to carry out procedures, and that central to this was going to be the use of manipulatives, representations and intelligent practice. This decision was made in 2015/2016, but the curriculum itself wasn't implemented until September 2018, and then only for the Year 7 pupils (11-year-olds) beginning in that year (before being rolled out in subsequent years as this year group progressed through the school).

Those intervening years were spent developing the team in key areas, alongside designing, refining and sequencing the programme of study and then collectively creating the lesson materials for it. Even after the initial rollout, we kept working on it, spending departmental time each year in reviewing the lesson materials for the upcoming units of work (led by the teachers who had written the materials) to ensure that all teachers understood the key points behind them. This leads me on to the next thing to consider.

You are never done

A curriculum is, by definition, an ever-evolving beast. Whether it is minor tweaks or major revisions, there will always be ways to improve it. In our implementation of the latest Key Stage 3 curriculum at Brockington, we realised after a couple of years that one of the units needed to be changed as it was taking too long, and the pupils were getting confused and bored with the unit content.

This meant creating a new unit with some of the content from the previous unit, re-sequencing the Year 7 content and redesigning some of the teaching materials to fit with the new sequencing. We also spotted that some of the multiple-choice diagnostic questions didn't have suitable incorrect responses to really interrogate the misconceptions that pupils may have at various points in their learning, so the team went back and amended some of the options.

Assessment

Another crucial element to include in your thinking around the curriculum is how you know it is doing what you want it to do. One of the major ways you will judge this is using assessment.

Assessment thinking has to accompany curriculum thinking; it is impossible (or at least highly inadvisable) to separate the two. Designed well, assessment and curriculum should work together and complement each other, with the curriculum specifying the material to be taught, assessment helping to indicate how effective that teaching is and the curriculum being modified in light of the results of the assessment, with the effect of the modifications then being further assessed and so on.

Now, much of this will happen in lessons and will be the responsibility of the teacher (although you may be responsible for making sure teachers are skilled enough with assessment for learning to do this). However, there will be points across the school year when groups of pupils will be completing centrally set assessments at broadly the same time. Whether we are talking about teacher assessment in class or centrally set departmental or school assessments, if we want to make the best use of them, we need to think about the following issues.

Are the inferences we can draw from the assessment valid?

Whether designing your own or using assessments provided from elsewhere, it is important that we understand what a pupil's ability or inability to answer an assessment question tells us about how their understanding compares with what we were expecting. Take, for example, this assessment question:

Find the perimeter of this triangle:

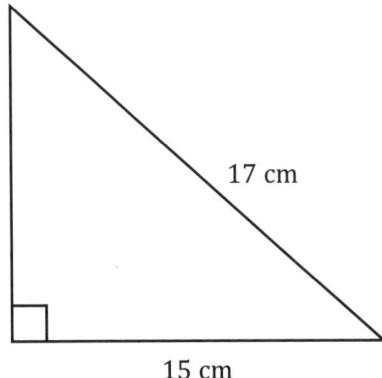

If a pupil answers this question incorrectly, we may conclude that they don't know Pythagoras' theorem, and so might decide to allocate further time in the coming lessons to reteaching Pythagoras or, alternatively, to set the pupil extra homework to review and complete more Pythagoras questions.

However, lack of knowledge of Pythagoras' theorem is just one possible reason why a pupil may answer this question incorrectly. It may be that they know Pythagoras' theorem but didn't recognise that it was necessary in this case. It may be that they knew Pythagoras' theorem was required but applied it incorrectly (in this case, likely something like $\sqrt{15^2 + 17^2}$ to find the third side). Examining the answer the pupil gave might allow us to make a more valid inference about their knowledge, but it definitely isn't the case that an inability to answer this question automatically leads to a clearly diagnosable problem.

In her book, *Making Good Progress? The Future of Assessment for Learning*, Daisy Christodoulou talks in detail about valid inferences.[7]

Can we use multiple-choice questions to help with the diagnosis of problems?

One way we can help to set up questions in order to make valid inferences from them is to give a limited number of options for the correct answer. Consider this revision to the question above:

Find the perimeter of this triangle:

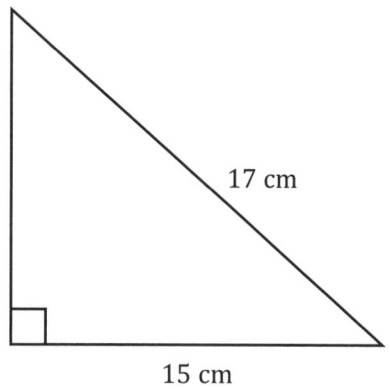

A: 32 cm   B: 40 cm   C: 54.7 cm   D: 60 cm

In this case, each answer allows us a relatively secure inference about how the pupil has gone about the question:

> A: The pupil has simply added the two lengths, demonstrating that they have some idea of the perimeter requiring added lengths but not necessarily about total length.
>
> B: The correct answer, suggesting that the pupil is comfortable with the necessary mathematics to answer the question.
>
> C: This is as a result of the thinking from the previous point (namely, that the third side of the triangle can be found as a result of the calculation $\sqrt{15^2 + 17^2}$. We can infer that the pupil

---

7   D. Christodoulou, *Making Good Progress? The Future of Assessment for Learning* (Oxford: Oxford University Press, 2017).

has a relatively secure understanding of perimeter, as they know to find the third length in the triangle before summing, but is still insecure in their understanding of how to apply Pythagoras' theorem.

D: The most likely way that a pupil arrives at this answer is that they correctly work out that the missing length in the triangle is 8 cm, but then applies the process for finding the area of the triangle ($\frac{1}{2}$ x 15 x 8), suggesting that the pupil is secure in applying Pythagoras' theorem but hasn't separated the concepts of perimeter and area successfully.

Of course, the biggest issue with multiple-choice questions is the possibility of the pupils guessing, which significantly impacts on our ability to draw valid inferences from the responses. To help overcome this, we can utilise a confidence weighting as part of the assessment. This could be a Likert scale (from strongly agree to strongly disagree, or similar) alongside the question (particularly if pupils are completing the assessment online) or a confidence-weighted template like the one below.

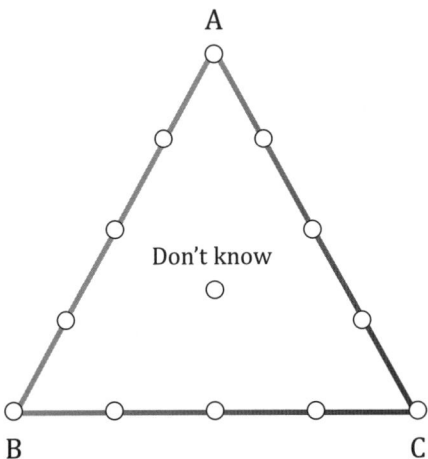

The pupils mark the circle which most closely corresponds to how they feel about their answer – for example, if a pupil is absolutely sure the answer is A then they mark the circle closest to A, whereas if they are unsure between A and B they would mark a circle somewhere along the line. The obvious drawback here is that you can only have three responses (the increase in complexity required for four responses makes it unsuitable for use with the vast majority of pupils). There is also the possibility that pupils will still guess, particularly as there is no penalty for being wrong here. However, we can fix this by using a scoring system like the one below (assuming the correct answer is A, as in this case):

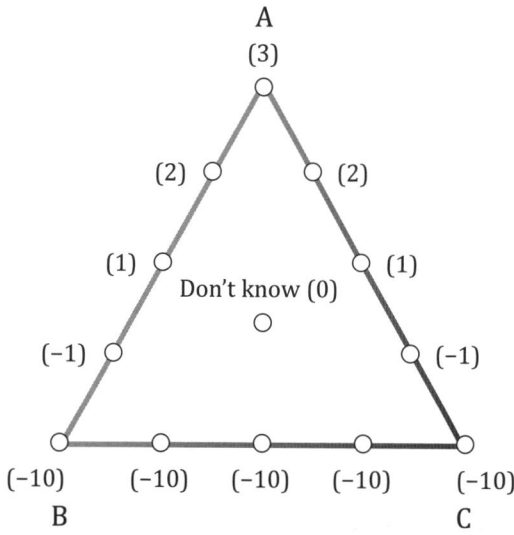

Provided pupils know that this is how the questions will be scored, the use of the negative scores makes it much less likely they will guess when they don't know. In addition, if a pupil does show extreme confidence in an incorrect response, we are likely to see the hypercorrection effect come into play.[8]

Do assessments revisit knowledge and understanding over time?

Whether or not you agree with the idea of learning as 'a change in long-term memory',[9] I think it is clear that when we teach pupils about a mathematical idea, we want them to retain that knowledge

---

[8] See Durrington Research School, The Hypercorrection Effect, Spaced Practice and Remote Learning (3 January 2021). Available at: https://researchschool.org.uk/durrington/news/the-hypercorrection-effect-spaced-practice-and-remote-learning. Blake Harvard has written about multiple-choice and confidence weighting on his blog: B. Harvard, Confidence Weighted Multiple-Choice Questioning, *The Effortful Educator* (22 June 2020). Available at: https://theeffortfuleducator.com/2020/06/22/confidence-weighted-multiple-choice-questioning.

[9] P. A. Kirschner, J. Sweller and R. E. Clark, Why Minimal Guidance During Instruction Does Not Work: An Analysis of the Failure of Constructivist, Discovery, Problem-Based, Experiential, and Inquiry-Based Teaching, *Educational Psychologist*, 41 (2006), 75–86 at 75. Available at: https://www.tandfonline.com/doi/abs/10.1207/s15326985ep4102_1.

and understanding over time. Very often, though, the only time that pupils revisit their knowledge of a concept is the next time they need to use it, which might be a year or more later in some cases. I know there are plenty of teachers out there who have suffered the soul-wrenching despair of having taught something to a group, only for all memory of it to have disappeared when you come to build on it at a later date. This is why interleaving and interweaving are an important part of curriculum planning; this also needs to be replicated in assessment design.

At Brockington, all our assessments are designed to be cumulative, so that questions from previously studied work are included alongside questions about the most recently studied concepts. This task isn't as onerous as it might first appear. If you are using question banks to build assessments, then this can be as simple as including questions that assess multiple units or leaving in parts of questions that refer to material taught earlier in the curriculum. Even if pupils aren't answering these questions correctly, the sheer act of asking them will prompt pupils to recall that they have studied this material previously and it will help when reteaching it.

Where is the time to follow up on the results of assessment?

There is no point in conducting an assessment of any type if there is no time available to correct the issues that it identifies. This is often referred to as a 'conveyor belt' curriculum model, where teaching takes place, pupils are assessed and then, regardless of the outcome, pupils are moved on to the next unit of work (with the assessment score or 'grade' recorded somewhere for posterity). This is how externally set examinations such as SATs or GCSEs work, of course, but the purpose of these tests is fundamentally different to what we should be trying to achieve through assessment (again, Daisy Christodoulou's book explores the differences in some detail[10]).

It is virtually impossible for a school to assign any sort of grade to a pupil's assessment in anything approaching a reliable process, and, typically, assigning a grade doesn't help the pupil to improve on any gaps that the assessment reveals. What does help is clear feedback on how the pupil can continue to develop from the knowledge they

---

10 Christodoulou, *Making Good Progress?*

have demonstrated, and then giving them the time and support they need to action that development. This means that our curriculum must include space for issues arising from assessment to be tackled, even if it comes at the expense of complete curriculum coverage; ensuring that pupils see 'all the curriculum' is no good if they aren't actually learning from a lot of what they are seeing.

How are teachers going to use the results of assessment beyond helping pupils to improve?

Teachers, departments and subjects have to report to all sorts of stakeholders – senior leadership, governors and parents. This is likely to become even more high profile in maths given the recent (at the time of writing) announcement about the 'Parent Pledge' where schools will be required to inform parents/carers when their child is 'behind' (whatever that might mean) in maths or English and explain how the school is addressing the gap.[11]

What we report is often driven by the results of the assessments we carry out, but the form of reporting is often not under our control. For example, many secondary schools mandate the reporting to parents of predicted or 'working at' GCSE grades as early as the first report a pupil receives in Year 7 (age 11). Whilst it is pretty much impossible for a department or subject area to do this in a reliable way, this doesn't stop the stakeholders requiring it! This is something that the subject lead needs to consider when committing to an assessment strategy, so that the generation of report data is as straightforward for teachers as possible, whilst still allowing the assessment to serve its primary purpose of informing teachers as to where pupils need further support to progress.

---

11 HM Government, *Opportunity for All: Strong School with Great Teachers for Your Child* [white paper]. CP 650 (March 2022), ch. 3. Available at: https://www.gov.uk/government/publications/opportunity-for-all-strong-schools-with-great-teachers-for-your-child.

Feedback and marking

In the last two points above, I have touched on a couple of areas related to assessment – namely, feedback and workload. As maths lead, you may or may not be in a position to determine how feedback works for your subject; it will depend on school policies and procedures around feedback and marking and how much leeway individual subjects have to interpret these. In my last role as head of department at Brockington, I worked based on the following principles.

Marking for accuracy isn't generally a good use of teachers' time

Many questions used in maths teaching require pupils to produce accurate results to problems. Where this is the case, it seems to be a no-brainer to ask pupils to peer- or self-assess these tasks. It may take two or three minutes of class time to ensure the pupils know exactly what they are looking for, but this is definitely time well spent for two reasons.

Firstly, pupils will almost certainly learn more from engaging with any mistakes that they or their peers have made if they are checking them in the moment rather than having to engage with a teacher's comment at a significantly later time. Secondly, even if the teacher review takes only 10 seconds for each pupil, for a class of 30 pupils this is five minutes, which is approximately twice as long as the time taken in class. This isn't time efficient in terms of teacher workload.

Although prompt feedback is highly impactful, it doesn't need to be written down

Clearly, if pupils are going to improve their understanding of mathematics, then they will need feedback on how they are progressing along the way. However, I would happily postulate that the most prevalent form of feedback – writing comments in pupil's books – is the least effective approach in mathematics. Unless pupils have a strong routine around acting independently on written feedback, interpreting it and knowing how to follow it up, then it is likely to be processed and forgotten very quickly.

What has much more impact is either:

- **Feedback given whilst pupils are working.** This can come in several forms. It may be the teacher circulating and identifying issues they can tackle individually with a single pupil or several pupils. It might be breaking tasks down so that accuracy checking happens throughout (rather than lots of answers given only at the end of the task). It might be through the use of numerous example-problem pairs in succession,[12] so that pupils can check after each problem that they are on the right track. This sort of feedback is typically much more impactful that written feedback.

- **Whole-class feedback following task review.**[13] As teachers who have to leave written feedback will no doubt have experienced, much of what we write for pupils is very similar. This isn't particularly surprising if we think about it. If we judge that most pupils have reached a point where they can handle learning about a particular mathematical concept, and they all receive broadly the same experience, then we should expect the results of any tasks we set them where they are applying this learning to be broadly similar as well, which will mean that our feedback to many pupils is also going to be along the same lines.

    Of course, writing duplicate comments in 30 pupil books isn't a particularly good use of teacher time. Instead, tackling these problems collectively by making the whole class aware of any common issues or any particular successes and then working on furthering the concept together not only saves a lot of time for teachers but is generally going to be more useful for pupils too. My standard practice would be to choose the assessments and tasks that are going to provide me with the most useful information about pupils' learning at that point, review them and then revisit any areas that have been problematic for the majority, whilst signposting where further support is available.

---

12 See https://berwickmaths.com.
13 See https://macstandl.com/whole-class-feedback.

Even if marking and feedback policies aren't within the control of the subject leader, what is important is that you use any power you do have to interpret these (and other) tasks in such a way that they will maximise the impact on pupils whilst not wasting teacher time. Most teachers I know don't mind working hard, providing they know that the work will be impactful for pupils and that there is no other way they could have the same impact more efficiently. In being responsible for the strategic leadership of maths, this is something we must always have in mind in everything we ask teachers to do.

Maths in other areas of the curriculum

Of course, the mathematics classroom isn't the only place where pupils are going to encounter mathematical ideas. Pupils will come across maths in many different subject areas, from formulae in science to graphs in geography to isometric (called orthographic) drawing in design and technology. In leading maths across a school, you should pay attention to how and when pupils are going to encounter your curriculum ideas in other subjects or at other times, and work with your fellow subject leads to try and make this experience as coherent as possible. Some people take this to mean that they need to drastically rearrange the maths curriculum to ensure that pupils don't get 'taught it wrong' in another subject. Now, you may be able to restructure your maths curriculum to bring in certain concepts early enough such that pupils can transfer the knowledge to other subjects, but care must be taken that this isn't at the cost of a coherent maths curriculum.

What is arguably more important is that you and your team are aware of where mathematical concepts may have already been broached in other subject areas, so that you can use this to your advantage, or at least highlight where there are similarities and differences. For example, many science departments use formula triangles to tackle problems involving compound units or simple proportional/inversely proportional formulae, whilst their use in maths classrooms seems to be fading. I always explain to pupils that this is because the goal in science is to solve some simple problems involving these concepts, but in maths they need to learn a lot more about the concepts themselves as well as tacking more challenging problems.

But it is only the fact that I am aware of these areas that I can even have this sort of conversation in the first place and that my team can do the same. The list of possible areas is quite long across the primary, secondary and tertiary sector, so rather than try to produce an exhaustive one here, I recommend that you talk to your other subject leads (or nominate a member of staff to do it – more on this in the next chapter) about where concepts like proportion, geometry, graphicacy and so on appear in their curriculum.[14]

Key points

- A lot of time needs to be invested in curriculum planning and changes, both in terms of research and development as well as collaboration and team preparation, if you want to see the most impact.

- A good maths curriculum is an ever-evolving entity that adapts as pupils' needs change.

- Assessment is an integral part of curriculum and needs to be planned alongside it, including time to adapt based on the results.

- What teachers must report, and the form this takes, needs to be considered in conjunction with assessment.

- Feedback must be as impactful as possible on the pupil, whilst being as time efficient as possible for teachers.

- Be aware of where mathematical ideas are explored in other curriculum areas and how you can use this effectively.

---

14 I have previously written some advice for subject leads on promoting numeracy across other curriculum areas, so I won't replicate that here – see: P. Mattock, Five Ways Maths Teachers Can Persuade Secondary Colleagues to Embed Numeracy, *TES* (4 April 2017). Available at: https://www.tes.com/magazine/archive/five-ways-maths-teachers-can-persuade-secondary-colleagues-embed-numeracy.

Chapter 5

Subject time and development

In Chapter 2, we looked at the importance of dedicating subject meeting time to the improvement of mathematics teaching. In terms of professional development that has the greatest impact on pupil outcomes, sustained subject-specific development comes near the top of the list.[1] As maths lead, you will need to look at how you want the curriculum and teaching to move forward in the long term, design a programme that will ensure your staff understand the journey you want to take them on, get them on board with the direction of travel and then actually make it happen.

This development programme should cover the following points.

Lay out the rationale for the change you wish to make

For people to support a development programme, they will need to understand why the change is necessary. For example, this might include sharing research around whatever practice you want to work on and discussing the implications of what the research suggests, or it might be some data analysis that highlights a key area for improvement. When I introduced homework booklets to Brockington College, it was simply a matter of showing staff what the benefits would be in terms of learning for the pupils and workload for the team.[2] It has to be obvious how this development is going to benefit the pupils without causing excessive work (and reducing it where possible).

---

1 M. Cunningham, Prioritising Subject-Specific CPD in Your School, *SecEd* (13 November 2019). Available at: https://www.sec-ed.co.uk/best-practice/prioritising-subject-specific-cpd-in-your-school.
2 See https://www.tes.com/teaching-resource/brockington-college-maths-homework-booklets-11223661.

Make sure staff are clear on what they are trying to achieve, not just want you want them to do

Teacher agency is an important part of professional learning.[3] Teachers are much more likely to apply themselves fully to improvement work if their own expertise is recognised and they have the opportunity to make meaningful decisions about how their own and others' practice improves. When we were working towards the implementation of a new scheme of work at Brockington College, the issue I kept coming back to was wanting pupils to understand mathematical structures, not just follow procedures. Because staff understood the end goal, as well as some of the approaches that could help to achieve it, they could make decisions in their planning and contribute effectively to team discussions around the materials we were producing.

This isn't to say that explicit direction isn't useful or required; again, in that scheme of work development, there were some very clear practices that all staff needed to undertake, but I also made sure that staff understood how they contributed to the end goal.

Allow time for experimentation, reflection and adaptation

An ongoing programme of practice development requires teachers to try out new ideas, reflect on their success (or otherwise) and adapt to improve. Time needs to be built in for teachers to do this both individually and collectively. Plan for time in subject meetings for staff to share their experiences, discuss any issues they have had and find solutions to them. Where possible, time should also be made for teachers to plan together and watch each other working on whatever idea you have asked them to implement.

When planning a series of development, you might find it useful to have a template for the planning, like the one on the next page.

---

3   L. Calvert, The Power of Teacher Agency, *Learning Forward*, 37(2) (2016), 51–56. Available at: https://learningforward.org/wp-content/uploads/2016/04/the-power-of-teacher-agency-april16.pdf.

What is the activity setting and timing?	Who is involved in this activity?	What activity will take place? What resources are needed?	How does this activity contribute to the end goal?	How did it go? Do you need to adapt any of the future plans?
After-school departmental meeting (September)	All department staff	Review use of procedural and conceptual variation in task design. Examples of intelligently designed practice.	Proper use of intelligent practice should highlight mathematical structure to pupils.	
Classroom-based paired work (September/ October)	All department staff in pairs	Staff will co-plan tasks that use one or both of procedural and conceptual variation and teach whilst the other observes. Ideally two cycles to be completed.	It will help staff to embed the use of variation theory in planning.	
INSET time (October)	All department staff	Staff share examples of co-planned tasks and reflections following observation cycles. Time needed to discuss issues and how they might be resolved before the next cycles.	It will help staff to embed the use of variation theory in planning.	

As well as time spent on the development of subject priorities, it is also important to provide support for individual staff priorities. In Chapter 1, we considered opportunities you might want to take up to help you prepare for a leadership role. Now you have the role, you need to make those opportunities available to your team (assuming you have the scope to do so). Not only will this mean that you aren't having to directly implement every initiative, but it will also provide valuable professional development for members of your team. We will address appraising others in Chapter 11, but in terms of distributed leadership you should consider the following points.

Talk to your team members about their ambitions

There will be some individuals in your team who are aiming to take steps into leadership. Some will want to go down the route of developing others without taking on additional leadership responsibilities. Others will want to concentrate all of their energies on their own classroom practice. Others still may be in the early stages of their career and might have ambition but need to focus on improving their teaching first. Understanding how your team see their future will allow you to offer them appropriate opportunities to pursue their goals.

Decide which things you need to do

There will be aspects of your role that you will feel need to be under your direct control; these will depend on the nature of your role and the school in which you work. Then there will be other responsibilities for which you will need to retain oversight but won't feel the need to manage day to day. These are the opportunities you can offer to your team. For me, these tasks included mentoring ITE students, planning the after-school intervention programme (although I did that during the first couple of years at Brockington as both the school and my team were new to Key Stage 4 delivery), running enrichment clubs for pupils interested in extra-curricular maths, and being responsible for ordering and equipment. In addition, my second-in-charge would manage one key stage (including data analysis, intervention planning and so on) and things like corridor displays.

Discuss the level of support people need

All of your staff should be contributing to the teaching and development of your subject area. For classroom teachers (in England at least) that might be through teacher standard 4: 'contribute to the design and provision of an engaging curriculum within the relevant subject area(s)'[4] or, for teachers on the upper-pay range, their 'achievements and contribution to the school [should be] substantial and sustained'.[5] However, to do so, staff will need differing levels of support. Some will be happy to agree a task or contribution they can make and then go away and get on with it, only coming back to you to demonstrate the finished article. Others will require more support along the way.

For example, someone in your team is organising a mathematics trip. If they have run trips in the past, they may only come back to you when all the paperwork is ready for you to check and sign. If they haven't run a trip before, they may need guidance from your educational visits coordinator and you may need to help them with setting short-term goals for key milestones before the trip is fully planned, writing permission letters (if the school doesn't have a standard letter for trips) and so on. Discuss this with staff before they take on the management of the task, so you are both clear on what is expected.

It was always my general practice to offer opportunities openly at first and see who expressed an interest in them before any further discussion. Whether you do this or prefer to be a little more targeted will likely depend on your team and how you see their strengths and areas for development. It will also potentially change as you grow into the role; you may feel you need to hold on to certain opportunities in the early years that you may choose to pass on as you gain more experience.

---

4 Department for Education, *Teachers' Standards: Guidance for School Leaders, School Staff and Governing Bodies* (July 2011; updated June 2013 and December 2021), p. 11. Available at: https://assets.publishing.service.gov.uk/government/uploads/system/uploads/attachment_data/file/1040274/Teachers__Standards_Dec_2021.pdf.
5 National Education Union, Performance-Related Pay for Teachers (25 July, 2022). Available at: https://neu.org.uk/advice/threshold-progression-and-upper-pay-range.

Underperforming staff

Of course, development isn't always about moving your subject team into new practice or supporting the ambitions or aspirations of a team member; sometimes it is a necessary step as they aren't meeting the Teachers' Standards. Although the decision around the level of mandated support will come from the head teacher (that is, whether the teacher requires informal support, formal support or capability), as the subject lead you may well have a role to play in organising or providing that support (or both). In this case, it is crucial that you remember the following points.

This is about support, not judgement

The best outcome from any level of support is that the teacher improves to the point where they no longer need help to maintain the Teachers' Standards. This is always the aim. Your job in this scenario may be to help identify and agree the specific tasks that the teacher needs to do in order to meet the standards, or it may simply be to help them with the actions that are going to be required to get there. You might need to assist with planning, or to observe and help develop questioning approaches. Eventually, you might have to advise your head teacher on whether the teacher has met the goals that have been set out for their improvement, although the ultimate judgement and decision will come from them.

Keep records and follow up

Whilst the goal is definitely to support the teacher to improve, there will need to be evidence of that improvement which will help the head teacher to decide on the next steps once the period of support is concluded. For their sake as well as yours, every aspect of the support you provide should be documented and followed up with the teacher. I found it best to put everything in an email, which serves as a good narrative of what you have worked on with the teacher (and I always asked others involved in the support to do the same and copy me into the email).

So, if I observed a lesson and discussed it with the teacher afterwards, then the fact that I had observed and the actions we had agreed as a result would be sent in an email to the teacher. If we had met to discuss planning and devised a list of important points for them to include in their planning, then the fact that the meeting had occurred and the list would be sent in an email. As well as providing a clear picture of the support the teacher has received, this is also beneficial for them as it gives them clarity over exactly what they need to do to demonstrate they are making the necessary progress towards the goals that have been set.

Keep your end of the bargain

Any support plan involves agreements from both the teacher and those tasked with supporting them with regard to what the support is going to look like and what improvements are expected of the teacher as a result. If you are the person (or one of the people) tasked with providing part of the support, you must meet your side of the agreement. If you don't provide the support you have agreed, then you cannot expect the teacher to make the necessary progress. And if they don't improve, then pupils' mathematical learning will ultimately suffer.

Learn more about coaching and mentoring

Much has been written about the use of coaching and mentoring in education, so it isn't a good idea for me to rehash it all here (whole books have been written about both).[6] Needless to say, they are the two main approaches used in working one-on-one to support and develop staff and both have a valuable part to play. Making sure you have a thorough understanding of coaching and mentoring, and which one is more likely to lead to improvement and success on

---

6   See, for example, J. Beere and T. Broughton, *The Perfect (Teacher) Coach* (Carmarthen: Independent Thinking Press, 2013); Northern Territory Principals' Association, *A Guide to Support Coaching & Mentoring for School Improvement* (Camberwell, VIC: Australian Council for Educational Research, 2016). Available at: https://research.acer.edu.au/cgi/viewcontent.cgi?article=1012&context=professional_dev; and H. Hughes, *Mentoring in Schools: How to Become an Expert Colleague* (Carmarthen: Crown House Publishing, 2021).

which occasions, is very important in supporting all of your team but particularly those individuals who need to make rapid progress.[7]

As a maths subject lead, one of the biggest pressures you are likely to face is around the results of externally set assessments. We will examine this aspect of the role in the next chapter.

Key points

- Ongoing professional development around subject-specific pedagogy is some of the most impactful on pupil performance.
- Staff need to be clear about where you want the team to get to, so they can add their own expertise in getting there. They also need time to reflect and adapt.
- Offering development opportunities to your colleagues can be great for them and reduce your workload.
- When supporting underperforming staff, keep records and meet your commitments, but don't judge.

---

[7] The Northern Territory Principals' Association define coaching as 'the nature of the processes and the type of communication used to help another person realise his or her personal or professional goals' and mentoring as 'relationships where more experienced individuals (e.g. school principals) share their skills and knowledge with other, less experienced practitioners': *A Guide to Support Coaching & Mentoring for School Improvement*, p. 12.

Chapter 6

Dealing with results

No other subject in the school curriculum faces the pressure for performance that maths experiences. It is not only considered a core subject that is essential for post-16 progression, but also one that parents and carers simultaneously value very highly and yet often have difficulty in supporting both practically and figuratively (how many times have we heard parents say they were never good at maths?!). Add to this the pressure of school accountability and league tables, and there can be a lot to deal with when it comes to the results of government-mandated assessments. This situation is further exacerbated by the fact that most maths leads teach only a small proportion of the pupils actually taking the exams.

The important point when dealing with this pressure is to manage how much of it makes its way down to the team and the pupils. The right amount of pressure can ensure optimum performance,[1] but too much pressure and the strain will take them past peak performance. So, make sure that staff are aware of key performance targets (and revisit them regularly) and have to account for how they are trying to meet them, but don't keep harping on and on about targets every week or at every meeting.

Where possible, try to let your team manage the pace. This can be as simple as asking them how things are going with a target. If they say, 'Yep, fine, no worries,' then four times out of five leave it at that. On one of the times, perhaps ask just a couple of simple follow-up questions. If at any time they say, 'Actually, I'm struggling with …' then this is the time to go deeper on the issue they are raising and the target more generally.

When it comes to the children, make sure teachers are following up with pupils and parents where there might be underperformance or where more support is needed. However, ensure they understand

---

1 J. Carrier and J. Stewart, Episode 16: Resilience, *World of Work* [podcast] (2019). Available at: https://worldofwork.io/2019/02/performance-and-pressure.

that the pupil might be putting themselves under huge pressure already, so they might actually have to relieve some of it to get the pupil back to peak performance.

Hopefully, your results will meet or exceed expectations, and continue to do so. Even if they do, you will still be expected to see where improvements can be made; there are always areas to be developed even when results are good as a whole. Some of the areas you can look at are explored below.

Important subgroups

The most common subgroups are:

- Disadvantaged/pupil premium/free school meals pupils
- Pupils with special educational needs and disabilities (SEND)
- Gender
- Ethnic groups
- English as an additional language
- Prior attainment

The key here isn't just to consider the groups but the crossover between groups. For example, simplistic analysis might show there is an issue with the progress of pupils with SEND, but further analysis might show that these children are part of a wider problem with disadvantaged pupils. There might be an indication that there is an issue with boys' attainment, but a bit more digging might show that it is actually lower prior attaining boys who are struggling. Whilst you still need to guard against spending too much time for too little gain, delving just a touch further may save you from wasting time on the wrong areas.

Content and skills

As well as different subgroups of the pupil population, you will also want to look at different parts of the curriculum that have been assessed and find out if there was underperformance in any of these areas (bearing in mind what was said in Chapter 4 about drawing valid inferences, particularly from the types of questions you get in summative assessment).

A couple of years ago, an analysis of the feedback we got from our exam board suggested that Brockington pupils weren't answering the questions aimed at Assessment Objective 1 as well as pupils in other schools. This led to a member of our team doing some work to try and improve pupil outcomes in this area as part of a national professional qualification (NPQ).[2] (Due to the COVID-19 pandemic, we weren't able to test this with actual exam results but we did gather evidence of improvement in this area in mock exams.) Whilst it is always tricky to take end-of-year summative assessment analysis and apply it to other year groups, you might find a clear indication that an area of your curriculum isn't doing the job you would hope and so can amend the teaching of this in the future.

Classes and teachers

It is always worth investigating how classes compare in terms of residual measures (how well the class did in maths compared to other subjects), progress measures and/or attainment measures. However, you will need to bear in mind that residuals tend to be higher for higher prior attaining pupils (that is, if you set your classes by attainment then higher set classes will normally come out with a greater residual than lower set classes) and progress tends to be smaller for higher prior attaining classes. As they start at such a high level, they don't tend to make progress above the expected level.

The best way to use class-level analysis is to compare classes that are broadly similar in terms of prior attainment. This can tell you whether a teacher is performing particularly well (and therefore may have insights to share with other members of the team) or not so well (and therefore may be in need of extra support). Over time, class-level analysis may also indicate the key strengths and weaknesses of individual teachers. Do you have a teacher who always produces excellent results with high prior attaining pupils (above what you might expect) but doesn't do nearly as well with lower

---

2 See https://www.gov.uk/government/publications/national-professional-qualifications-npqs-reforms/national-professional-qualifications-npqs-reforms.

prior attaining pupils, or vice versa? Do you have a teacher whose pupils do great on the arithmetic papers but not so great on the reasoning papers?

Of course, we have to temper this with how much of the performance can be attributed to the teacher (how long has the teacher had the class?). But, like all data, its role is often to point us in a direction of further investigation rather than give us the full picture of what is going on.

Attendance

Attendance is a crucial factor to examine, but it is often missed by maths leads because it isn't data that is specific to maths. However, attendance is one of the key drivers of performance; if attendance of the cohort (or a subgroup) is low then this will always affect outcomes.[3] For large cohorts or subgroups the simple attendance figure is fine, but with smaller groups it is worth trying to get hold of the session attendance data. Just because a pupil was in school doesn't mean they attended lessons regularly.

Responding to poor results

A further pressure can come when results aren't what we expected (or are as expected but still not good enough). This can be a uniquely demoralising experience for you and your team, especially because you know that it is likely to lead to increased scrutiny and work for at least the next year or so. However, it is important not to give in to despair but rather to trust in your ability, take proactive steps to improve the situation and show your leadership team that you are the right person to lead your school to better maths results. In order to ensure you are on the front foot during the coming year, you should consider the following areas.

---

[3] Department for Education, *The Link Between Absence and Attainment at KS2 and KS4: 2013/14 Academic Year. Research Report* (March 2016). Available at: https://assets.publishing.service.gov.uk/government/uploads/system/uploads/attachment_data/file/509679/The-link-between-absence-and-attainment-at-KS2-and-KS4-2013-to-2014-academic-year.pdf.

Understand the stories of the year just gone

Having conducted your analysis of all the elements outlined earlier in the chapter, and having identified where there is underperformance, you need to put some time into figuring out why that was the case. If the underperformance was across the whole cohort, was it caused by an aspect of the curriculum? Was it school wide and beyond just maths? If it was underperformance of a particular class, were there staffing concerns? Was there an attendance issue with these pupils, either during lessons or at whatever supporting intervention you had in place outside of lessons?

Every result, down to the individual child, good or bad, has a story behind it. The more you know about the story, the easier it is to talk intelligently about it, which will give your SLT, governors or other external scrutineers the confidence that you have recognised the relevant issues and are on top of them.

Take an honest look at the next cohort

You may have had a group of pupils who underperformed in the last cohort, but that doesn't necessarily mean that this pattern will continue in the next cohort. If underperformance was due to poor attendance of a key group, look at the attendance of the analogous group in the next cohort. If there isn't an obvious issue with attendance, then make this clear to senior leaders (although, always say that you will be monitoring it carefully over the course of the coming year – and make sure you do).

Before planning lots of changes and interventions, make sure you take the time to compare the new year to the old. Each cohort of pupils is different, so identify the differences before you do anything drastic. Look back at unit assessment results, mock exams, reports data or whatever else you have to see how your cohorts compare, so that any changes you do make not only address the issues from the past but also have impact in the future.

Be ready to make the tough calls

If you have identified problems, be prepared to make the tough decisions required to make the necessary changes. If it means swapping a teacher from one class to another, then be prepared to sit down with that teacher and explain why you feel it is necessary. If it means modifying a certain approach or strategy – or even if it means doubling down on something that hasn't paid off yet (but you have evidence that it is starting to and will in the future) – then make that clear to the team (and SLT) and be prepared to put measures in place to ensure that it will be properly monitored and implemented.

This is the time when you might have to be slightly more autocratic in your leadership approach, although you should ensure the team understand the situation and listen to any ideas they might have to improve things. This is also the time when less experienced staff may look to you for answers or to get them out of the hole they perceive themselves to be in. Having a coherent plan that you can justify is essential in making sure that it is you, and not anyone else, who drives the agenda for the next year and brings confidence back into the team.

Show humility and be conciliatory

You have done your analysis and come up with your action plan, great, but don't go in seeming like you have all the answers and no one else needs to concern themselves with it. By all means, be assertive in what you believe, but also be prepared to really listen. Remember, your senior leadership also want the best for the pupils in your school and have valid experience they can offer to support you. I appreciate that in some schools the advice or actions of the SLT can be misguided, which can lead to a lot of extra stress and workload for you and your team, but the way to tackle this is rarely by being stubborn, particularly when you are coming off the back of a hit.

If possible, a good way to deal with this problem is to turn anything the SLT want to your advantage. For example, if they decide they are going to push knowledge organisers, can you make them complement something you are going to put in place anyway? If not, can you persuade them to allow something like a Frayer Model instead?[4] If your SLT want weekly assessments, can you use something like Diagnostic Questions, which are quick and straightforward to implement and might actually tell you something useful?[5]

If it really isn't possible to turn whatever it is to your advantage, can you reach a compromise rather than finding yourselves at loggerheads? If you go in with the attitude of 'my way or the highway', when it is clear that your way alone hasn't had the initial success you might have wanted, then you will probably find that your team's practices will be increasingly mandated and scrutinised by your line manager and other members of the SLT to ensure they have confidence in the actions that are being taken, even if you don't.

Whether we like it or not, results and accountability are a staple part of our education system for the present time, with maths under particular scrutiny no matter what part of the sector you work in. Being able to approach a set of results, good or bad, and deal effectively with the consequences is an important part of the work of a maths lead.

A difficult set of results isn't the only difficult situation a maths lead will face over the course of their time in the role. The next chapter will look at some of the other challenging scenarios you might come across and how you might deal with them.

Key points

- Whether results are as good as, better than or worse than expected, make sure you dig down into the analysis and find out where the real issues are.
- Particular themes to investigate in data analysis are key subgroups, how pupils have performed on your curriculum content areas, the performance of classes/teachers and the attendance of pupil groups.

---

4 See https://www.frayer-model.co.uk.
5 See https://diagnosticquestions.com.

- If there is a need for significant improvement, make sure you take the time to understand the story behind the results of the year just gone, and how applicable the same story is to the year to come.

- If changes need to be made, then sit down with colleagues and explain what is needed and why, but be strong and persevere with what you believe is necessary.

- Be prepared to listen to your SLT and work with them to implement both what you see as essential to generate improvements and also what they might see as being required. If you disagree with their objectives, look for ways to use this constructively or try to find compromises that might be acceptable rather than digging your heels in. Remember that members of your SLT have probably been through the same situation you are going through now and so might have valuable insights (or at least shouldn't be dismissed out of hand).

Chapter 7

Difficult situations

There are many challenging situations that can arise with a team who are teaching maths. Depending on your role, this may be your issue to resolve or it may be that of your pastoral or senior team. We have already alluded to many of these problems, including the underperformance of a team member, parental concerns or complaints, supporting with the behaviour of a difficult class and dealing with a difficult set of results.

In addition, we might also encounter challenges relating to the personal lives of our team, such as uncooperative members of staff or individuals with difficult home situations, and professional difficulties, such as how to manage split classes or non-specialist teachers.

The uncooperative teacher

A maths lead might have to deal with a team member who, either intentionally or unintentionally, isn't approaching the teaching of maths in a way that fits with your vision or curriculum intent. This can be trickier to handle than the underperforming teacher, as they might be able to make a case that whatever they are doing is 'working'.

The first step is to work with the teacher to modify what they understand by 'working'. It may be that pupils can follow step-by-step instructions but aren't being given the opportunity to develop their mathematical reasoning and problem-solving skills (if this is an area of your intent). It may be that pupils are being given lots of open-ended and exploratory tasks but without the underpinning of the explicit teaching they need to support them in making the most of these opportunities. In whichever way the teaching isn't aligned with your vision/curriculum intent, you need to try and impress upon this teacher the importance of collective effort towards a common goal. Teachers are typically team players, so if you can help them to understand that this is a direction the team is moving towards together then they are more likely to come on board.

Of course, it may well be that the reason the teacher isn't working in the required way is that they lack the requisite skills or knowledge to do so. This should become apparent in the conversations you have with them, and often manifests as defensiveness or other obstructive behaviour (similar in many ways to pupils, where 'I can't be bothered' or 'I don't like this' is often synonymous with 'I can't do this'). A key part of the conversation with a teacher who is misaligned with your departmental vision has to be around any support they might need to realign themselves. Perhaps they aren't confident in modelling the problem-solving strategies you want your team to be deploying and could benefit from some joint planning or lesson study in this area. Perhaps they need help with understanding the explicit teaching that underpins some of the open-ended tasks that are being used across the department and would profit from being involved in some departmental professional development time where this is discussed and drawn out collectively. Giving teachers a voice in this process is important and will generally translate to better results.

However, should the teacher still not fall into line, you will need to have a more difficult conversation with them. A teacher who isn't working in a way that is aligned with your team's ethos and approaches can damage both the experience of your pupils and of your team, neither of which should be underestimated. The teacher is unlikely to be carrying a cohort of pupils through their entire time at your school, and if the other teachers who will pick up these pupils or classes are having to redo (or, even worse, undo before they can redo) this teacher's work (in terms of supporting pupils to attain certain knowledge or skills), then this is going to create unrest within your team as well as disadvantaging the pupils.

If you can't get buy-in from a teacher, no matter how you try to approach them and persuade them, then you definitely need to do two things:

1   Inform your line manager and SLT of the difficulties you are having with this team member.

2   Set clear instructions for what you want this teacher to do, including how you expect to see this translate to the classroom and a timescale for implementing the changes. If this is done in person, then follow up with an email so there is an unambiguous record of it.

Ultimately, a teacher's refusal to follow specific instructions can be a disciplinary issue. Your line manager and head teacher will become involved if it starts to go down that route, and this will require firm evidence of actions requested and taken before this point.

All of this assumes that your vision or curriculum intent goes beyond pupils merely attaining the highest possible results and making the best progress. If that isn't the case, then it may well be that you won't come across this issue, as the only way a teacher wouldn't be aligned with the curriculum intent is if they are underperforming, in which case you would probably approach it in a similar way to that outlined in Chapter 1.

Personal issues

The personal life of staff can present significant problems in their working lives. If you work in maths leadership for long enough, particularly in a role where you are the line manager for a significant number of people, you will probably have to support individuals who are going through a life-altering illness, divorce or the break-up of a long-term relationship, bereavement and all sorts of other personal issues that can affect their ability to work well and productively. Very often, this will lead to absence, underperformance or an inability to follow the curriculum specified (due to lesson planning being affected).

However, care needs to be taken as you won't necessarily want to approach this situation in the same way as you would in other circumstances. For example, even if a bereavement leads to a planned absence, it would seem extremely callous to expect someone to send in cover work. If a member of staff is struggling with their health (physical or mental), which means their planning or lesson delivery isn't quite up to their usual standard, the last thing you want to do is exacerbate their condition by putting pressure on them to improve.

A lot of this comes down to knowing your staff: are they the type of person who can handle a brief conversation about an area of concern whilst they are coping with whatever it is that is going on? Even so, it is worth remembering that people under high levels of emotional stress might not behave in the way they would normally. In these sorts of scenarios, it is always my preference to simply let them know (and reiterate when necessary) that I am there to support them, and then to keep monitoring the situation, intervening only when it is clear that circumstances have become unsustainable (being very aware that a good teacher operating below their usual level of proficiency is likely to be better than a cover teacher, if they end up having to take a significant leave of absence).

If the situation does become untenable (for example, if a class is falling significantly behind because their teacher is giving them any old task to complete as they aren't able to keep their planning in line with the curriculum), then it is important that the ensuing conversation is as supportive as possible. It should focus primarily on what support the teacher needs in order to reach an acceptable standard, whilst making it very clear that you recognise this is a temporary phase for that teacher. As far as possible, try to keep the emotion of the situation separate from the functional elements.

In my experience, teachers going through personal turmoil can see the impact it is having on their work; they simply don't have the headspace or motivation to change things by themselves. Similarly, the vast majority of people with whom I have worked who have been in this situation appreciate having an honest conversation about it, providing it is handled tactfully and due respect is paid to their circumstances and usual high standards. If the problem isn't addressed in an appropriate way, then the teacher is almost certainly going to reach the point where they are absent or on an occupational health plan, which will be dealt with at senior leadership level. In this scenario, you must make sure you know the details of the plan in order to support the teacher and their class(es) effectively, and to keep the leadership of the school informed about any issues that arise.

Split classes

Another difficult situation that can arise in secondary maths departments (and also at primary where there are part-time staff) is classes that are split between teachers, and how best to approach the curriculum under these circumstances. Generally speaking, there are two ways this issue can be tackled:

1. Divide the units in your programme of study between the teachers, so that each teacher is responsible for the entire delivery of part of the curriculum.

2. Ask the teachers to deliver the curriculum between them, so that one teacher picks up where the previous teacher left off.

There are pros and cons to both of these approaches. The first is definitely simpler in terms of implementation: the units can be divided between the teachers at the start of the year and each teacher can plan independently of the other and at their own pace. However, this system may be harder on the pupils as they are having to switch between learning two different ideas and spend less time each week exploring and working on each of the ideas. This will be particularly tricky if your curriculum is sequenced so that each unit follows the previous one, especially if teaching materials include planned opportunities for interweaving and interleaving. However, the second 'follow-on' approach creates more work for staff as there has to be strong communication between the teachers to ensure there is coherence for the pupils.

Emma Sheppard outlines some of the factors that she sees as important when working with split classes (whilst advocating for the divided units approach),[1] of which I will highlight three:

- **Communication.** As we have seen, this is absolutely key in making either system work, but particularly the continuous curriculum approach. If you are going to ask your teachers to work in this way, then you might need to consider how you can support with scheduled communication. This can be simplified if you already have centralised teaching materials, in which case, a teacher only needs to keep their partner informed about where they are up to with the materials (which they will

---

[1] E. Sheppard, Five Ways to Make Split Classes Work, *TES* (24 June 2021). Available at: https://www.tes.com/magazine/teaching-learning/secondary/five-ways-make-split-classes-work.

normally be able to do via email) as their colleague won't need as much time to plan the next lesson as they would if planning from scratch.

- **Consistency.** Whilst each teacher will have their own foibles when it comes to running their classroom, pupils will benefit from an element of uniformity around how the lessons are approached in terms of content and style. Again, centralised expectations can help with this (we deliver a centralised expectations lesson to all Brockington pupils at the beginning of Year 7), as can time for teachers to collaborate on some joint expectations prior to the start of the year (although this may not be possible if you have a number of split classes, particularly if they involve the same teacher).

- **Equity.** No matter how a class is split, whether relatively evenly or heavily weighted towards one teacher, there will need to be planned equity in the workload that is expected of each teacher. How will you split assessment and feedback? Homework? Parents' evenings? This can be even more difficult if you have several split classes and they involve the same teacher and the same year group.

For example, this year we have a new teacher who is the majority teacher (in terms of time) of four of our Year 7 classes and a minority teacher in another class. Clearly, this individual cannot be responsible for the majority of the assessment, feedback and homework of four classes and the minority in another class and be the lead teacher for four classes at parents' evening (there wouldn't be enough appointment slots). The head of maths and I have already looked at how we can distribute the parents' evenings between the staff more equitably (in one case, the minority teacher will lead the parents' evening for that class). Likewise, our systems for homework, assessment and feedback have made it much more manageable for teachers, so that it can be split over the course of the year.

Whilst Sheppard advocates for split topics when teaching split classes, and my preference is generally for continuous curriculum teaching due to the nature of mathematics, I will add that there is nothing wrong with splitting the planning of the topics between teachers, even if the delivery is continuous. Where centralised planning isn't already in place, working with teachers to share the planning between them (if there is more than one split class you will need to ensure that no duplicate work is going on), so they don't have to plan from scratch at short notice, will drastically improve how they feel about split classes as well as their general workload.

The management of non-specialist staff

The final difficult situation we are going to discuss is the management of non-specialist staff, particularly at secondary school. Currently, there are simply not enough maths teachers actively seeking employment to cover all the vacant maths teacher positions that exist in England. This means that many schools are turning to non-specialists to teach maths lessons, and maths leaders are having to integrate and manage staff who are inherently torn between their teaching roles.

Whilst some non-specialists will commit to developing their mathematical knowledge, others will simply be trying to get through the lessons with as little work as possible in order to concentrate on their 'main' job. This doesn't mean that non-specialist teachers will go out of their way to be substandard, simply that their lack of pedagogical knowledge combined with their lack of passion for mathematics compared to their main subject may mean that developing their approaches to teaching maths is lower down on their priority list. That being said, I have come across some excellent unqualified and non-specialist teachers who are truly committed to teaching mathematics as well as possible, accessing training, seeking out opportunities for joint planning, observing lessons taught by specialists and more besides.

Centralised planning and homework can help in this situation; not only can it can provide a lesson framework for non-specialist teachers to use but it can also make clear the subject knowledge they are expected to teach. Other good ideas include:

- **Agree the structure and timings of departmental meetings.** If your non-specialists are part of two (or more) departments, then agree with the other departmental head(s) about how you are going to structure your departmental meeting time. Maybe you are going to timetable the relevant maths work for the non-specialist in the first half of the meeting, and then the non-specialist teacher can go to their usual department for the second half (or vice versa). Maybe you are going to trade off, so they come to you for one meeting and then their regular subject for the next. However you decide to structure things, it is always advantageous to put a plan in place.

- **Consider splitting the classes.** While splits are generally something we want to avoid, in the case of accommodating a non-specialist it may be better to deliberately split two classes. In this way, all the pupils get some specialist time rather than having one class taught completely by a specialist and the other by a non-specialist. This also means that the specialist can support the non-specialist.

- **Ensure the non-specialist is dealing with in-class admin.** In my school, homework is marked in class once per week. If there is a split class with a non-specialist, then the homework will be due in one of the lessons taught by the non-specialist teacher. Similarly, we will try to ensure that lessons where pupils are completing assessments fall to the non-specialist (our assessments leave enough time for them to be marked in class), which the specialist can then review and feed back on. Anything that relies on general rather than subject-specific pedagogy should be planned for the times when the non-specialist is leading the lessons, so that when the class is being taught by the specialist they are actually benefitting from their subject knowledge.

There are a few other challenging situations that a maths lead may face during their career, but as these are more involved we are going to be dealing with them in separate chapters. We will turn to the first of these, adding to your team, in the next chapter.

Key points

- If a teacher's practice isn't in line with your curriculum vision or intent, make sure that they understand why this is important, that they have the knowledge and skills to bring their practice into line and, if all else fails, that they have been given clear verbal instructions followed up in writing.

- If a teacher's personal life is in turmoil, make sure they know that you are there to offer any support they need and, where necessary, to be open and honest about any issues with their work. However, consider the timing of these conversations carefully and keep them solution focused to try and remove any emotional considerations, as well as recognising the temporary nature of the situation.

- When dealing with split classes, it is important to work with the teachers to ensure effective communication, a consistent approach, coherent curriculum and equitable workload.
- If you have non-specialists who are working between departments, then work with the other departmental head(s) to ensure fair access to their departmental meeting/INSET time, so they can get access to key messages and training.
- Consider splitting classes to limit the impact of non-specialist time. Make sure any in-class admin is dealt with by the non-specialist, so that all specialist time is spent teaching maths.

Chapter 8
Adding to your team

The amount of influence you will have in appointing new members of staff will depend on the nature of your role. In primary schools, recruitment is often the near exclusive realm of the SLT and governors, whereas in secondary schools (and beyond) a maths department lead would generally be part of the interview process, including on the panel itself. Whilst you will rarely get too much say about the programme or interview questions (which typically have a relatively set format in order to ensure fair processes), it is nonetheless an important opportunity for you to ensure that you are bringing in the right person.

Whether you are replacing a staff member who has moved on or adding to your team due to expansion, aim to address the following questions.

> Does this person share your vision for mathematics teaching (or are they at least happy to help you realise it)?

The last thing you want is to appoint someone who is pretty much guaranteed to create a difficult situation for you by not following your lead when it comes to your curriculum vision and intent. I always try to get some time on the interview day to meet with the candidates collectively to discuss how we work as a team. This allows anyone who doesn't like the sound of our approach to withdraw from the process (it is important to remember that the candidates need information to decide whether this is the right role for them too) and gives you a chance to see who is enthusiastic about what you are saying and who is more reticent about it. This might be a time set aside during the day or it might be just over lunch or a break, but having this conversation is a crucial part of the day.

Can this person work with young people?

I wouldn't appoint someone who was going to cause problems with respect to the team's way of working, no matter how good they were with young people, but neither would I hire someone who wasn't going to be able support pupils in learning mathematics. Given that mathematics is a subject that a significant number of pupils find challenging, I would always look for someone who can get the children working for them, even when those same children aren't hugely enthused by the subject matter.

I will look for clues during the lesson observation. These are a standard part of the interview day, and as the maths lead I would always want to be part of it (although, if we have a lot of candidates I might not be able to see them all). In some schools, the preference is to observe the candidate in their school rather than ask them to teach in yours, in order to see them with a class with whom they have established themselves and to get a more natural view of their practice. If this is the case, I would definitely want to be on that visit. However, I would prefer to observe them in my own school, so I can see how they work with our pupils and how they begin to establish their way of working (which is arguably more important for someone taking on a new role).

Does this person know maths well enough?

Given a choice between a candidate with a high level of maths knowledge who struggles to work effectively with young people and a candidate who works really well with young people but who may need some support with their mathematical knowledge, I will typically take the latter. It is easier to support someone in gaining subject pedagogical knowledge than it is in the skill of relating to and managing pupils. Others may disagree, and that is fine. However, we need to keep in mind that this person will need to teach maths classes and will need enough maths knowledge to do so effectively. If needs be, classes and timetables can be managed to ensure the new teacher isn't out of their depth with regard to subject knowledge before we have had time to support and develop it.

Is this person committed to the idea of learning?

The inimitable Mark McCourt has commented to me on more than one occasion that teachers should be 'towering intellects', a sentiment with which I thoroughly agree. To me, this means teachers who are committed to their own as well as their pupils' learning. This includes professional learning, an area that is often overlooked by teachers, but that I believe is a fundamental part of being a professional educator. However, it also extends to the idea that teachers should be 'learned people' who can converse with their pupils on a variety of scholarly topics, showcasing and potentially inspiring pupils to become those same well-educated adults they see around them.

Will this person integrate well with other team members?

In addition to being able to build relationships with and enthuse young people, any new teacher will also need to work well with the other members of your team. Ideally, an interview day will include time for the candidates to meet with existing team members, even if it is just over break or lunch, and give you a chance to observe how they interact. Are they friendly with the team? Do they seem happy or put off by the sorts of things they talk about or how they socialise? (It may be a good idea to prime some of your team to discuss previous social outings or events to see how the candidates respond.)

As well as whether they will get on with the team, you also need to consider whether their skills will complement those of your team. If you have a group of very experienced teachers, do you want to add some youth and fresh ideas? Do you need someone who might have experience of mentoring? Someone who can improve the use of ICT across the team? Of course, these factors aren't a deal breaker, but preferably you want someone whose skills and knowledge will supplement those of your existing team.

Appointing teachers

As previously mentioned, as maths lead you won't have much (if any) control over the process for interviewing other maths teachers. However, you will have some control over (at least in the secondary sector or higher) the class and lesson the candidates teach. It will, of course, depend on the day and time of the interviews as to what classes are available. The interview lesson may be for part of a lesson ('Teach for 30 minutes on …') or it may be a full lesson.

There are different schools of thought on this. Some people will opt for a topic the pupils haven't seen in the past (but have the prerequisite knowledge for), such as the next lesson in the planned sequence. The rationale for this is that it needs to be something the pupils genuinely won't know, so there can be an assessment as to whether they have actually learned anything during the lesson. However, there are a couple of drawbacks with this approach. Firstly, if the lesson isn't up to scratch, then it may make it more difficult for the regular teacher(s) of that class to unpick what has happened and reteach it, so that it is well understood (as well as potentially taking up more curriculum time than one would like as the content will have to be taught again). Secondly, pupils may struggle to give an honest reflection (assuming they are going to be asked about it) about the lesson as they have no experience of being taught that content against which to measure.

The clear alternative is to ask the candidates to teach something the pupils have learned about previously. This will, of course, negate the two points above: the pupils should already understand the subject matter well enough that the quality of the interview lesson should have little bearing on their experience of the content, and they should be able to talk reasonably intelligently about how the teaching of the content compares with how they were taught about it previously. The (hopefully) obvious downside is that it is more difficult to judge whether the teaching has had any impact.

However, if learning can be thought of as 'an alteration in long-term memory' (at least according to the 2022 Ofsted School Inspection Handbook[1]), then it follows that we probably can't judge if anything meaningful has been 'learned' during an interview lesson. What we can judge are whether the things are in place that can lead to

---

1   Ofsted, School Inspection Handbook (updated 11 July 2022), pt 222. Available at: https://www.gov.uk/government/publications/school-inspection-handbook-eif/school-inspection-handbook.

learning – that is, planning for the introduction of new material in a coherent way using clear modelling and interspersed practice, and lots of questions to check for pupil understanding (at least if you subscribe to Rosenshine's research[2]). For this reason, I would generally prefer to have candidates plan and teach a lesson that pupils already have experience of. Whether you subscribe to this view or not, the important thing is that you have a clear idea about what you want to find out from the lesson observation, and how (if necessary) you are going to compare the candidates' approaches to the lesson.

Appointing to leadership roles

In many secondary or higher departments, the maths lead isn't the only person of responsibility within the maths department. I have seen or worked in departments where there is a second-in-department or where there are leads for each key stage in the school. In my current school, there is a second-in-charge and a teaching and learning responsibility (TLR) holder in charge of whole-school numeracy who works with the head of mathematics. When looking to appoint to a position of responsibility, there are other things that need to be considered.

- **Their understanding of leadership approaches.** We discussed different styles of leadership in Chapter 2, and it is important that new TLR holders have some familiarity with how to lead people effectively. Even if they don't know the six widely recognised styles of leadership, it is important that they have some knowledge of the different ways they might need to work with their team to lead any initiatives for which they are responsible.

- **How will their skills and experience complement your own and any other TLR holders?** This is very similar to how any new member will integrate with the team (described above). This new person (or current team member) is going to be part of the department leadership team, so there is little point in appointing someone who doesn't bring anything new to the team. Sometimes, this means you might have to modify the roles within your team. When appointing my latest second-in-department, I could see that their skills and

---

2   B. Rosenshine, Principles of Instruction: Research-Based Strategies That All Teachers Should Know, *American Educator* (spring 2012), 12–19, 39. Available at: https://www.aft.org/sites/default/files/Rosenshine.pdf.

particularly their passions were very similar to my own (unsurprising given that we had worked together for years). This meant that I shifted my focus and priorities to enable them to take the lead in the areas that were best suited to them, whilst also ensuring that they took on other responsibilities outside of their comfort zone.

- **What support will they need to carry out their duties effectively?** Whenever we appoint someone to a position of responsibility at my school, we always ask this question during the interview and then actually listen to the answer. Some people can readily identify gaps in their knowledge that they will need help to fill, whilst others will feel ready to get stuck in immediately with little formal support.

  Once someone takes on a TLR role within your team, the best bets are regular meetings and careful monitoring. Although they may have been delegated responsibility for a particular area, ultimately you are the lead for maths and are still accountable for all the work that goes on. You will need to meet with your TLR holders regularly, so you can understand how they are progressing in the areas where they are leading and find out whether they are having an impact. You may have an action plan that you can monitor (we will look at action planning in Chapter 10), which may include what support will be required to carry out the plan. Having specific actions to focus on is really helpful to get at the heart of what support a TLR holder requires to be successful.

Having explored the scenario of adding to your team, the next situation we will investigate – which impacts all maths leads – is external monitoring and scrutiny, most commonly by Ofsted.

Key points

- Make sure you have time to talk to the candidates about how your department approaches maths teaching, so you can see how they react and so they can understand what they are signing up for.

- Focus on whether the candidate has the right characteristics: do they enjoy working with young people? Are they committed to learning for themselves and others? Arguably, this is harder to 'train' than subject knowledge (although clearly they need enough subject knowledge to be credible).
- Consider the candidates as part of your team: who is going to fit in both socially and with regard to complementary skills?
- Think about how you can use the selection of class and lesson that the candidates will teach to give you the information you need about their teaching practice.
- When looking for other leaders within your team, examine what the candidates know about effective leadership, how their skills and passions will integrate with you and others in your team with responsibility, and how you will need to support them with their role.

Chapter 9

Ofsted and inspections

Whatever your opinion of Ofsted (or the other bodies that inspect schools across England, the rest of the UK and abroad), school inspection is a reality in many places. As a core subject, it is more than likely that a school inspection will involve looking at the curriculum and teaching and learning of maths. Currently, under Ofsted, this takes the form of a 'deep dive' into the subject (we will explore this in more detail below).

What inspectors look for when reviewing a school is governed by the framework for inspection. In England (at the time of writing), Ofsted's inspection framework last had a major update in 2019 to focus its attention more towards the strength of a school's curriculum[1] – what a school wants its young people to gain from their studies and how it goes about ensuring this happens. This (for many welcome) shift from using excessive amounts of school outcome data and graded lesson observations towards a focus on tracking and triangulating pupils' experience of the taught curriculum has potentially increased the role that middle leaders will have in the inspection process.

I remember my last inspection as a head of maths under the old framework (and the one before that in a different school). My main input involved ensuring the team were ready for any lesson observations they might face; meeting with the inspectors in a group of three heads of subject to be asked generic questions about the school's treatment of its middle leadership with regard to professional development, support and so on; and collecting examples of pupils' work so the inspection team could examine the quality of the books.

---

1 Ofsted, Education Inspection Framework (updated 11 July 2022). Available at: https://www.gov.uk/government/publications/education-inspection-framework/education-inspection-framework.

In contrast, during my school's most recent Ofsted inspection (in 2022), my successor as head of maths had a nearly hour-long conversation with one of the inspectors and then accompanied them on a 'learning walk' of the maths lessons going on at the time, during which the inspector talked to pupils and looked at their work. Further examples of books from these classes were taken for scrutiny. In addition, there was a meeting between the inspector and all of the teachers whose lessons had been visited at the end of the school day – not to receive feedback on the lessons (as was the practice under the previous framework) but rather to be asked questions about how the department was run and how curriculum plans from the subject leadership were implemented.

The point of this, of course, is to highlight that what you, as a maths subject lead, will have to prepare for will depend entirely on which Ofsted framework is in operation at the time. Whilst the latest inspection framework is purportedly 'evidence informed', even at subject level this does not make the framework immune to significant overhaul in future years. (Ofsted are publishing reviews of the research they use in each subject area to inform their framework, such as the mathematics research review.[2]) There are two reasons for this: firstly, the conclusions Ofsted have arrived at based on the review of the research (particularly in mathematics) are still very much contested,[3] and, secondly, whatever research is used to inform the framework, the focus may change depending on the prevailing thinking of the day.

I say all of this as a bit of a health warning. This chapter will include a mixture of thoughts and advice specific to the current Ofsted framework and about contending with inspection more generally. Therefore, depending on when you are reading this, some information may be a bit antiquated (although it is at least preserved for posterity!).

---

2   Ofsted, Research Review Series: Mathematics (25 May 2021). Available at: https://www.gov.uk/government/publications/research-review-series-mathematics/research-review-series-mathematics.
3   See, for example, J. Carr, Ofsted Maths Review 'Needs to be Withdrawn', Experts Warn, *Schools Week* (9 July 2021). Available at: https://schoolsweek.co.uk/ofsted-maths-review-needs-to-be-withdrawn-experts-warn.

The deep dive

One of the biggest differences in the 2019 inspection framework was the introduction of the 'deep dive'. Contrary to what some may think, a deep dive isn't a subject inspection. Rather, it follows on from the top-level discussion that inspectors have with the SLT prior to the start of the inspection during which they try to get a picture of what senior leaders think and say about their curriculum. Several deep dives are then carried out into different subject areas to see how this vision (intent) is translated into subject-specific curricula. Not surprisingly, maths is often chosen for a deep dive as it is almost guaranteed to be taught to multiple year groups during the course of the inspection (at least in primary and secondary schools) and, of course, as a core subject, it will typically come under scrutiny in some guise.

As a subject lead for maths, when the call for an inspection comes in, you should be ready to undergo a deep dive. This will usually consist of the following four aspects:

1 **A meeting with an inspector focused on the mathematics curriculum.** The inspector will ask a series of questions that will allow them to get an understanding of why your curriculum is designed and sequenced in the way it is, including why you have chosen to teach certain content at certain points and why you have chosen to place some content before or after other content. In maths, this will include assessing whether pupils are covering the full national curriculum.

2 **Visiting lessons with an inspector focused on the implementation of the outlined curriculum.** The key thing here is that the inspector wants to see those points you have talked about in the meeting actually happening in the classroom. For example, if you have stressed the importance of mathematical thinking, then this should be evident in the lesson visits; even if it isn't present during the inspection itself, they will look for evidence of it in books and through talking to pupils. They will also want to see that you, as the subject lead, have a handle on how your teachers are progressing with the curriculum. A typical question asked at this point is: 'Tell me what I should expect to see during this lesson/learning walk?'

3. **Work scrutiny and pupil voice.** These will be conducted alongside each other. As subject lead, you will be present during the work scrutiny, so the inspector can discuss with you what they are seeing and how it ties in with your earlier conversation. You won't be part of the pupil voice as the inspector won't want pupils' responses to be influenced by your presence. The books/work used for the scrutiny will usually belong to pupils who have been part of the classes observed, and it is these same pupils (or a subset of them) who will be used for the pupil voice.

4. **Staff voice.** The inspector will want to speak to the teachers they saw as part of their earlier learning walk. This discussion will have two main purposes. The first is to ensure that the detail of the curriculum intent that you shared with the inspector in the initial meeting can be articulated by the staff – that is, the teaching staff understand how what they were teaching fits within the sequence you have outlined, where it is leading and what they have taught beforehand that prepared their pupils for the learning that was intended today. You will only be present for this part of the meeting if you yourself were observed teaching during a learning walk. Even if you are present as maths lead for the first part of the meeting, you definitely won't be present for the second part. This is when the inspector will investigate how you, as the subject lead, support the development of staff with regard to their mathematics teaching, and also how you ensure that the workload doesn't overburden teachers and that you actively look for ways to reduce this burden.

Fortunately, the aide memoire materials used as part of the training that inspectors receive to conduct deep dives were leaked in 2022.[4] These are an invaluable tool in ensuring that you are well prepared for what the inspectors will be trying to determine when they deep dive maths.

---

[4] P. Coffey, Ofsted Crib Sheets Explainer: Training Guides for Ofsted Inspectors Now Free for All Schools, *Third Space Learning* (2 December 2022). Available at: https://thirdspacelearning.com/blog/ofsted-crib-sheets.

Preparation

The number one tenet when facing inspection as a maths lead is that if you take care of your team, then they will take care of you. Of course, this is good advice for all year round, but it is especially true the night before an inspection. This is when staff will be on edge and working hard to try and make sure that any i's are dotted and t's are crossed. You will have important tasks to do as well, but you must make sure your team have everything they need. For me, the night before an inspection generally goes as follows.

1. Whole-team meeting

Invariably, at the end of the day before the inspection begins, there will be a whole-staff meeting led by the principal. Afterwards, I will talk briefly with my team, just to ensure they are all clear on our priorities and have what they need for the following day. Rather than feel frustrated, everyone with whom I have worked has appreciated the extra support and clarity offered by this meeting (provided it doesn't take too long).

I will remind the team of key curriculum messages, our approach to maths teaching and learning, assessment, feedback and so on. I will check in with what content each of them is teaching over the next couple of days and ask whether they need any support in terms of planning or resourcing. I will also anticipate any anxieties – for example, that a certain pupil may cause issues or they aren't sure how they should respond to a pupil with a particular question or problem. I will reassure them that I believe in their practice and the work we do, and tell them where I will be available if they need anything (and until when).

I will also remind everyone that they don't need to stay late to put on a 'good show' for the school; some people prefer to work (assuming they have work to do) in the comfort of their own home, whilst others will want to stay at school until they feel completely prepared for the next day, so when they go home they can switch off. Either is fine, and the team needs to know this. If a number of people are staying on, you might want to think about organising some food for them.

2. Visiting the team individually

A little while after the whole team meeting breaks up, I will always make a point of touring the department and catching up with everyone individually (at least those who are still in the building). There may be matters that a team member prefers to discuss with you privately or has occurred to them while they have started preparing for the next day. Even if they don't have any questions, it is nice for them to see that you are making time for them and have their needs as a priority.

3. Touch base with my SLT link

At some point in the evening, I will have a short catch-up with my SLT link about the department more generally. In all likelihood, they will track you down as they check in on the subject areas they line manage, but if they don't, I will make a point of seeing them in case they need anything specific from the subject area over the next day or two.

4. Deal with my own stuff

There will definitely be things you need to have ready in time for the following day. Even if Ofsted no longer mandate any particular paperwork, there will be bits you want to have ready for your own peace of mind. This may be related to your lessons, your curriculum (intent statements etc.), a department or school policy you want to review or something else. Whatever it is, make the time and deal with them. At my current school, this would be copies of seating plans, making sure books and resources are in the correct classroom (I am a mobile teacher who teaches across several classrooms) and reviewing where each year group are up to in their scheme of learning, so I am ready to talk about it the next day.

Inspection day

When it comes to the inspection itself, there are a few key details to remember.

Keep your leadership team informed

Your senior leaders will be keeping track of what is happening across the day, hoping to build a picture of what the inspectors are seeing and what threads they appear to be following, so they can be ready to react. If you or your team have any interaction with the inspectors – in lesson observations, discussions or anything else – then you need to make sure your leadership team are kept informed about what they have seen, what they have asked and so on. Ideally, you should find time to let them know in person, but if that isn't possible then send an email or note to keep them up to date. This applies whether you think the conversation or interaction was positive or negative; if an undesirable incident occurs, it is important that your senior team knows so they can decide how best to handle it.

Steer the conversation

The inspectors are only in school for a finite amount of time, and they can only spend a little of that time talking to you. While they will definitely have particular questions to which they want answers, you should take every opportunity to drive the conversation towards the areas you want to highlight. You can use the conversation as a vehicle to draw attention to any excellent practice in curriculum design or sequencing, lessons, books and so on. If you need to bullet point some notes and carry them around or take them to the meeting, then do so; the pressure of the situation may push details out of your mind, but it is crucial that you communicate everything you want to say.

Avoid overselling

Whilst you will want to direct the conversation to legitimate areas you want to emphasise, don't forget that the inspectors will attempt to triangulate anything you assert. For example, if you say that they will witness a recall activity at the start of every lesson, then as well as potentially asking you for the rationale behind this approach, they will also look for it in lesson observations, ask pupils about their experience of it in class and enquire about it with staff. If these elements don't line up with what you have said, the inspectors may conclude that you don't have as clear an idea about the practices used in teaching maths as you seem to or that you haven't communicated these properly to the team.

The best advice is always to be positive but honest in your conversations with inspectors. Highlight the good points and, where possible, avoid the bad. However, if sidestepping issues that aren't as good as they should be isn't possible, then be clear about what you have done and what you are doing to develop these areas, and where you still intend to go on that journey.

Key points

- Make sure you are up to date with the latest inspection framework and what Ofsted looks for in schools.
- Make sure your team are taken care of; they will take care of you in return.
- Be well prepared for any conversations you may have with members of the inspection team, so that you can drive the agenda – but remember to be honest!
- Keep your leadership team informed of anything the inspectors observe and talk about when they are looking at maths.

Chapter 10
Subject improvement plans and action planning

Every year (at least) as a maths lead you will find something that you feel needs to improve. This could be motivated by analysis of assessment, pupil or staff voice, access to research or the outcomes of inspection (to name but a few). There may also be issues that the school is looking to improve across all subjects which maths will have to work on as part of the wider programme of development. These are the sorts of areas that will be included in a subject improvement plan.

The point of a subject improvement plan is relatively self-explanatory. It is designed to capture the annual objectives you have for the development of the subject, and the process by which you will make them happen, so you can hold yourself to account for these developments over the course of the year. Your school may have a template for this (which may or may not match the one used for the school improvement plan), or they may be happy for you to summarise the planned developments in a way that suits you. Either way, you will probably want to consider the following aspects when writing a maths improvement plan.

Aims and objectives

Improvement plans are, ultimately, a strategy borrowed from the world of business and so will include similar features. A key aspect of business planning is to look at aims and objectives. Technically, the aims here will be very general in nature; in a maths context, this might be things like 'Improve the proportion of pupils achieving ...' or 'Develop approaches to teaching ...' The objectives will be much more specific details that work towards the aim. For example, if the aim is to develop approaches to teaching a particular aspect of maths, the objectives might include carrying out research, visiting other schools, leading development sessions, implementing a lesson study programme for this aspect and so on.

The objectives are the real heart of the improvement plan; they represent what needs to happen in order for your aim to become a reality. Without clarity around your aims and objectives at the beginning of your improvement plan, then the document is unlikely to help you drive development in the areas you have identified.

Ways of measuring implementation and impact

Alongside clarity in what you are trying to achieve, another key area where you need to be explicit is how you will know when each objective has been successfully implemented, including what impact towards the overall aim the achievement of the objective will have. These could be data driven (qualitatively or quantitatively) or simply a matter of actions having been completed.

Taking the earlier example, activities like carrying out research or visiting other schools allow for the gathering of different approaches towards teaching a particular area of maths, and so the measure of their implementation and impact is that they have been done and their influence factored into the later objectives. In contrast, leading a series of development sessions or implementing a lesson study programme around a particular area of maths are (hopefully) designed to lead to direct improvement in the classroom and consequently in pupil outcomes and experiences. This means that the measure of the implementation and impact of this sort of objective should be tied to the improvements you would want to see in pupil outcomes or, if experiences, through something like pupil voice.

Requirements involved for the objectives

Many objectives that lead to improvement will have requirements in terms of time, budget, materials and so on. Whilst these may change as the objective develops, it is still worth trying to determine what the requirements for each objective will be and planning for them

Subject improvement plans and action planning

ahead of time. This will also allow you to make sure you have adequate budget and time for everything you are hoping to achieve; if not, you will need to re-evaluate what is achievable.

Thinking about timing can also help to fix the order in which you might need to approach these objectives, or at least the timeframe in which the different objectives need to start. For example, if an objective around lesson study is going to take 20 weeks to come to fruition, then it needs to begin relatively early in the school year (assuming the aim is to complete it within the academic year). Furthermore, any research that is going to inform the design or implementation of this objective needs to take place even earlier. Considering details like these is essential in making sure you have the time and resources to make your improvements successful.

The people involved in implementing and overseeing the objectives

As well as the time, budget and materials required for an objective to be completed, staff will be necessarily involved in their implementation. Depending on the objective this could just be you, it could involve members of the SLT (particularly if the aim is tied to the school development plan), it might be other TLR holders in the department or it could be the entire team. A key point here is to identify any objectives for which others are going to take responsibility. This will be important in holding them to account for the completion of these objectives, as without them you won't achieve your wider aim.

In addition to the general subject improvement plan, there might be specific objectives or other aspects of the department that require separate action planning. This might occur when an objective needs to be broken down further or it may relate to something that comes up separately to the subject improvement plan. For example, I have used an action plan to help guide the improvement of a specific member of the team, for the development of whole-school numeracy (deliberately kept separate from the maths department improvement plan) and many other things besides.

The structure of an action plan isn't likely to be much different to a subject improvement plan. Fundamentally, they have the same role: to plan the steps to take you from your current situation to a better situation. The main difference is in their utility. A subject improvement plan is a continuing and evolving document that is regularly updated (at least yearly) to keep the teaching and outcomes of the subject moving forward. An action plan is used for tackling a specific issue that requires a detailed strategy in order to implement the necessary change. You should consider the use of an action plan where this sort of detailed documentation is required, particularly when you need to communicate and collaborate with others about the project in question. The Open University has a nice module on action planning (although, admittedly, the focus is on children's rights rather than schools more generally).[1]

Self-evaluation

Another important process of improvement or action planning is self-evaluation. Most schools will produce a school evaluation form, which may well be accompanied (or even informed by) a department or subject evaluation form.

A school, department or subject evaluation form will typically prompt leaders to reflect about different aspects of their area of responsibility in order to inform the improvement plan. These areas may be tied to the Ofsted framework areas (quality of education, leadership and management, behaviour and attitudes, personal development) or tied directly to the school or subject improvement plan. Whichever approach your school takes, and whether you actually have to complete a formal school evaluation form or not, it will be worthwhile reflecting on the following questions when you come to consider your school improvement plan.

What is the quality of the maths lesson experience pupils are receiving?

This is the most important question to answer when it comes to evaluating where maths teaching is in your school. You will know what you want the pupils' experience to be whenever they study maths in lessons, so how does what they are actually receiving measure up? Are there the expected opportunities for recall? For developing their reasoning skills? For working on authentic maths

---

1 See https://www.open.edu/openlearncreate/mod/oucontent/view.php?id=53774&section=1.3.

problems? Whatever it is you want for the pupils, you need a way of establishing the extent to which this is happening across the team. This will depend on your school's processes for quality assurance, but you may also have evidence from learning walks, lesson observations, work scrutiny or pupil voice. Consider this evidence dispassionately: what does all of this collectively tell you (and not tell you) about the quality of lesson experience pupils receive? If you can identify aspects that aren't as you would like them, then this may well be something to include in an improvement plan or to formulate an action plan around.

What is the quality of the experience that pupils receive for their out-of-lesson learning opportunities?

As well as what pupils are doing in class, we also need to try and gain a clear understanding of what pupils are doing outside of lessons. This includes homework, any out-of-class intervention or revision, enrichment activities, trips and so on. There will be records of attendance and completion that can shed light on this, as well as scores gained on homework or assessments that include material from the intervention or revision sessions. These should give you the necessary information to determine whether these strategies are having the desired impact and highlight any areas that need to be improved.

What are pupil outcomes like in all areas of your curriculum?

If your curriculum is set up well, and the quality of lessons, homework and so on is where it should be, then outcomes should be high across the curriculum. If this isn't the case, then it may be that one of these areas can be improved (see the caveat regarding disposition below). These days, the results of most statutory examinations are accompanied by a detailed breakdown of pupil performance across the different areas of the assessment, as well as providing analysis of the performance of different subgroups of pupils (e.g. disadvantaged, SEND). This detailed analysis should be studied carefully to highlight whether pupils are struggling in any of the assessment areas, which may need to form part of an improvement or action plan, or similarly, whether there are any groups of pupils who may need a different approach to ensure they are able to achieve as well as their peers.

Do pupils have the disposition to study maths?

However, it is possible that groups of pupils may experience difficulties in a particular area , and this isn't down to the curriculum or an intervention. It may simply be down to disposition. This links to behaviour and attitude in the Ofsted framework and is one of the five strands of mathematical proficiency.[2]

Bluntly speaking, learning requires effort (at least those things that are 'biologically secondary'[3]). You can have the most well-sequenced maths curriculum, high-quality teachers delivering excellent lessons, homework and enrichment practices – everything that should allow you to be successful – but this could be for nought if the pupils don't have a productive disposition towards study. It can be very tempting to treat this as a school-wide rather than a maths-specific problem (and sometimes it can be), but this doesn't mean that subject teachers don't have a role to play. Engaging pupils in learning is the job of every teacher, and whilst this doesn't mean making the activities that pupils do 'fun' at the expense of being genuine learning opportunities, it does mean that you may need to dedicate an action plan or part of an improvement plan to finding ways to engage pupils better in their mathematical learning.[4]

How is maths contributing to the whole-school development?

The school will have its own evaluation form and improvement plan, and as a core subject maths will always have a role in helping the school to achieve its overall improvement aims. It may be that part

---

[2] National Research Council, The Strands of Mathematical Proficiency. In *Adding It Up: Helping Children Learn Mathematics* (Washington, DC: National Academies Press, 2001), pp. 115–156. Available at: https://nap.nationalacademies.org/read/9822/chapter/6.

[3] D. Didau, Education Isn't Natural – That's Why It's Hard, *The Learning Spy* (23 February 2017). Available at: https://learningspy.co.uk/psychology/can-learn-evolutionary-psychology.

[4] For some ideas on how to do this see: R. Pearson, Making Maths Lessons Fun – Is It the Best Way to Encourage Learning?, *Third Space Learning* (19 November 2022). Available at: https://thirdspacelearning.com/blog/making-maths-fun-or-engaging.

of your subject improvement plan ties directly to the school improvement plan, and so by achieving that part of your plan you are also contributing to the school's aims. It may be that looking at the school evaluation form or improvement plan prompts you to think, 'Actually, I need to get the team working on ...' It is always worth coming back to whole-school improvement priorities and planning how your team will contribute to the overall school mission.

The most important factor when evaluating your responses to these types of question is whether your answers are accurate. When it comes to aspects of subject improvement, it can be very easy to say, 'It feels like we're here.' These feelings can be useful, but you also need to be wary of conflating what you feel with what you have evidence for. Establishing the true nature of a situation (as far as is practicable) is what allows for an open and robust plan to improve. Otherwise, you can have an excellent plan that ultimately doesn't lead to improvement because it addresses a problem that wasn't actually the problem you needed to address in the first place!

This fits with the GROW model for coaching (which is another vehicle that is used to promote improvement, only on an individual scale rather than across a department), in which GROW stands for goal, reality, options and will.[5] I first learned about the GROW model during my Middle Leadership Development Programme (a precursor to the National Professional Qualification for Middle Leadership, which itself is a precursor to the newer NPQs for leading teaching or leading teacher development) and have used it to good effect with other staff over the years. Equally, I have used it myself when considering department and subject improvement. What do we want? Where are we right now? What could we do to get from reality to goal? What will we do? The point is that the R step needs to be routed in evidence about the real situation, otherwise the W step won't get you to the G step.

Subject improvement isn't something that can be done alone. Although, as subject lead, you may have primary responsibility for overseeing the subject improvement plan, it will require the input and collaboration of many people for that plan to actually translate into reality. There are many different approaches you might take to

---

5   See https://www.performanceconsultants.com/grow-model.

get your colleagues on-board (some of which we have already discussed), but one we haven't looked at yet is the appraisal process. We will turn our attention to this in the next chapter.

Key points

- Be clear about your aims and how your objectives lead to meeting those aims.
- Develop well-defined ways of measuring the success of the implementation of your objectives and the outcomes they produce.
- Plan for the time, resources, budget and people who will be required to complete the objectives.
- Make sure improvement plans are formulated on the back of robust self-evaluation that uses strong evidence to identify the current reality of the subject impact.

Chapter 11
Appraising others

As the maths lead, you may or may not line manage other team members. This is quite typical in most secondary or tertiary education settings, and also possible in some of the larger primary schools. If you are line managing other staff, then you will generally have to lead the annual appraisal of their performance. This will include reviewing the teacher's performance against their yearly targets and possibly their general performance against the Teachers' Standards, as well as agreeing targets for the coming year.

Every school I have worked in has used different systems and processes for performance management. Some have used online systems like BlueSky,[1] whilst others use in-house electronic or paper-based systems. Some have insisted on targets based on the attainment or progress data of particular classes or groups, whilst others (and it appears this is an increasing trend) focus more on the development of the teacher – both those to be addressed school wide and those that have been identified specifically for the teacher in question (either by themselves or through the department's or school's quality assurance process).

Whatever systems and processes your school uses for appraisal and performance management, there are various factors that are worth considering when you are discussing targets with teachers, both for the previous year and the coming year.

Prepare for every conversation about targets

In an ideal situation, every teacher you are appraising has met the targets they had for last year and automatically agree with any new targets you might want to set. Unfortunately, very few situations are ideal. If the targets your teachers are working towards are challenging, then there is a small chance that some won't achieve the set target. Now that performance-related pay is well embedded

---
1   See https://blueskyeducation.co.uk.

(having been introduced in 2014[2]), teachers can be rightly nervous if there is an indication that failing to achieve a target will result in a lack of pay progression.

You will need to reassure them that this isn't the case, or, if it is the case, you will need to prepare for how you are going to justify your recommendation. (For clarity, the head teacher and governors/trust pay panel will make decisions about pay; you will make only a recommendation as part of the appraisal process.) The best advice here, if you are unsure, is to talk to your head teacher. They will be best placed to guide you as to what you can and cannot do within your processes, and what sorts of conversations you can have with teachers around pay.

In addition, if teachers don't think the targets you want to set are realistic (which can be the case if you are using data-driven targets, in particular) then they are well within their rights to refuse. Targets should be agreed with the teacher wherever possible; whilst they can be set against the teacher's will, they are entitled to have their disagreement noted, which makes the review process next to useless. So, if you want to stipulate a target that you suspect a teacher will be uncomfortable about, you need to prepare for how you are going to justify the need for this target and reassure them that it is achievable. This leads to the next point.

Focus on actions that the teacher can complete or has completed

When discussing targets, it is useful to focus on the actions a teacher has taken to try and achieve a target. These may have been specified as part of the target-setting process or they may simply be actions the teacher has documented themselves (or as part of a quality-assurance process). If a teacher has fallen short of a target, providing they have taken actions to try and achieve the target (which could reasonably have led to its completion), then clearly the fault doesn't lie entirely with the teacher.

Similarly, when setting new targets, it is a good idea to discuss and agree actions the teacher will take to ensure the target is met. The teacher's focus should then be on completing the actions in the

---

2 National Education Union, Performance-Related Pay for Teachers (25 July 2022). Available at: https://neu.org.uk/policy/performance-related-pay-teachers.

knowledge that this should take care of the target, and if it doesn't then they have at least worked in good faith towards its completion. Knowing that there is an agreed set of actions for which the teacher is responsible for reaching is the sort of compromise that can make teachers feel better about accepting an ambitious target.

Set targets or actions that will have a noticeable impact on pupils or the subject

By far the easiest way to ensure that targets are set that both you and the teacher will value and take seriously is to make them important, of which the absence will be noted. If the teacher can see that what you want them to accomplish will have real impact and benefit the pupils or other team members, then they are much more likely to be invested in it, and to a high standard. Similarly, you are much more likely to be invested in monitoring their progress throughout the year. This is harder with data-driven targets (which is just one reason amongst many why they are falling out of favour with schools), but development targets can be a powerful way of ensuring that any targets or related actions are a worthwhile use of the teacher's time and effort.

Review targets and actions on a regular basis

Most schools have at least one review period during the year where progress towards targets and the actions to meet them are checked and discussed. This is the minimum number of reviews required; depending on the target, more than one review may be beneficial. This allows you to ensure that your team is on track to achieve their targets, and where this may not be the case to discuss what the teacher needs to adapt about their practice or actions.

How this conversation goes will generally depend on the level of expertise and experience of the teacher. Those with greater expertise or more experience should be encouraged to find solutions to any issues themselves, with you acting in more of a coaching capacity to bring those ideas out of the teacher. For those without the required level of expertise or experience, you may find that they need more of a steer in terms of how to proceed. This might include suggesting different possibilities for the teacher to consider or directing them towards a particular path.

As well as target-setting, part of the appraisal process involves reviewing a teacher's performance against the expected standards. These may be the general Teachers' Standards or they may be adapted for teachers at different stages in their career – for example, early career teacher, established teacher or upper pay scale teacher. No matter what targets or particular areas for development a teacher is working towards, it is important that they continue to maintain the standards expected of all teachers and, in particular, those of their career stage. Again, in an ideal situation, this would be the case for all of the team every year, and so each year it would simply be a case of confirming this fact as part of the appraisal.

Barriers to progression

We have discussed approaches for working with underperforming staff – that is, staff who aren't meeting the general Teachers' Standards – in Chapters 5 and 7. However, the appraisal process goes beyond underperformance. It may be that you have a colleague who is looking to progress to an upper pay scale who isn't quite meeting the standards that the school sets for this progression. When an aspect of poor performance or standards potentially impacts on pay progression, you also need to consider the following points.

Address any problems at the earliest opportunity

As soon as you think there may be an issue with performance that means the teacher isn't meeting the standards set for them, you need to talk this over with them at the earliest opportunity. This might not be immediately, as there may be circumstances in the teacher's personal life that need to settle a little first (as discussed in Chapter 7), but it does need to be as soon as possible. A teacher won't be happy if you wait until the end-of-year review before raising an issue that is going to deny them progression up the pay scale.

You will almost certainly want to keep your head teacher or line manager apprised of the situation, so they can offer advice and support in the monitoring of the situation.

Be clear about what standards aren't being met, how you know and what you will need to see in order to be satisfied

This conversation needs to end with the teacher being clear about what they need to do to meet the standards that are expected of them. Remember, this might be a teacher who isn't meeting the general Teachers' Standards, but equally it might be a teacher who is looking to progress to an upper pay scale who isn't quite meeting the criteria the school has set for this progression. Either way, teachers need absolute clarity about how they are going to meet the necessary standards.

Keep the conversation about information and away from emotion

Any conversation in which you have to tell a teacher that they aren't meeting the required standards for a particular progression (or the Teachers' Standards in general) has the potential to be an emotional and upsetting affair for both parties. You have to be prepared for the teacher to become upset, angry, anxious – a whole gamut of emotions – and for the toll that an emotionally charged conversation may have on you. As far as possible, you need to take the emotion out of this situation and focus on the issues and how you are going to resolve them.

A handy tip is to avoid the use of words like 'but' or 'however', which generally come across as dismissive. For example, 'I understand what you are saying and it is important, *but* we need to address ...' may sound like you don't actually understand what they are saying or that you don't think it is important. It is likely to prompt the member of staff to circle back to what they have said previously, as they may feel that you haven't heard or validated their position.

A much better word to use in this situation is 'and': 'I understand what you are saying and it is important, *and* we need to address ...' This sounds much more like you are accepting and validating their feelings, whilst simultaneously steering the conversation back to the facts of the situation. Of course, you can't seem robotic about it or as if you are reading from a script or pre-planned speech; however, it is worth keeping in mind and training yourself to avoid using words like 'but' or 'however' in these sorts of conversations.

When it comes to your own emotions, the truth is that everyone finds different ways to handle this type of situation. You may need to go and sit quietly for 5 or 10 minutes afterwards. You may need to go and vent to your line manager. However you manage it, you will need to find strategies to help you take care of your own mental well-being when you are involved in emotionally charged conversations.[3] Never dismiss the harmful effect they can have on you.

The final point to make about appraisal is that, as far as possible, the teacher who is the subject of the appraisal should be encouraged to complete the majority (if not all) of the paperwork. This is their opportunity to really reflect on the previous year, assess progress with their practice and what they need to do to continue to move forward as an educator. Taking professional responsibility for their own development and performance is an important part of being a teacher. However, this has to come with agency; teachers need to feel they have a measure of control over such things in order to take responsibility for them.[4]

Part of your role in this – alongside the school's general ethos and approach to teacher performance and development – is to encourage your team to use the appraisal process to examine their pedagogy and its impact in detail, without fear of judgement, and to commit to actions that will improve those areas they have identified as needing more work. This might be development of their own teaching practice or supporting the development of others; either way, this will have the most impact if it comes from the teacher themselves. You may need to prompt their reflections, and perhaps help the teacher to adapt their thinking once they commit it to paper, but the drive behind professional development should come from the teacher.

---

3   See https://www.mentalhealth.org.uk/explore-mental-health/articles/looking-after-your-mental-health-teacher.
4   M. Priestley, Teacher Agency: What Is It and Why Does It Matter?, *British Educational Research Association* (3 September 2015). Available at: https://www.bera.ac.uk/blog/teacher-agency-what-is-it-and-why-does-it-matter.

Key points

- Make sure you prepare for appraisal conversations.
- Focus attention on actions, particularly those that will have an important impact.
- Make time to review targets and actions regularly and monitor completion.
- Address any issues as soon as possible, being clear what the issues are and what needs to happen to address them, without allowing emotions to dominate the conversation.
- Encourage teachers to take responsibility for their own appraisal and provide the agency to allow them to do so.

Chapter 12

Leading beyond your school

These days there are many people involved in leading and developing mathematics teaching and learning outside of their school or across multiple schools. There are maths leads across different multi-academy trusts, specialist leaders in education, teachers who work as specialists or work group leaders for the National Centre for Excellence in the Teaching of Mathematics supporting teacher development across their local maths hub (the last two of which I have been lucky enough to do myself).

Leading and supporting mathematics across multiple schools is fundamentally different to leading in one school. In a single school, you are uniquely accountable for the experience pupils access and the outcomes they achieve, whilst this is rarely the case in a role across multiple schools. You may have overall accountability for the results across the group of schools, or you may have no accountability at all and be working purely in a supporting capacity. Even if you do have overall accountability for maths across a group of schools, each school will have its own maths lead who is answerable for what is going on in that school and who will report to their own SLT, which means that you might not have direct oversight or responsibility for them. Consequently, leading or supporting maths across a group of schools generally demands a more collaborative approach than leading maths in a single school, even for those leaders who have a very democratic style of leadership in their own school.

Even in a trust lead role, where the individual school maths leads may be directly accountable to you, being overly autocratic with teachers who have worked hard to achieve their own leadership roles rarely leads to a good working relationship. Ideally, you want the school leads and teams to be motivated to implement your initiatives. To get that buy-in from leaders and teams you don't work with on a day-to-day basis, you should consider the following advice.

Reassure and settle any nerves or hostility

When you first visit a school that you are supporting, the maths lead is likely to be nervous and may even be overtly hostile. Unfortunately, the accountability regime of the last few years has made teachers and leaders inherently unsure about external oversight, which often makes them feel that those who are there to support are instead there to judge and report.

This can be particularly prevalent if a school or leader is struggling, and may be concerned that you are there to gather evidence to use against them in support of capability procedures. In this scenario, your first job is very often to tackle the emotions the school maths lead is feeling before you can start work on anything that will improve the mathematics meaningfully.

Being open and honest is important in this situation; one of the qualities that leaders respect and admire is authenticity. I would usually start by explaining that my only role is to support the leader in achieving their goals and to help them give the best possible experience to pupils. I would then encourage them to ask me any questions they might have about me or my role. Being transparent can go a long way to allaying fears that I am there to judge or critique them.

Focus on their priorities first

After an initial introduction with the school maths lead, it is a good idea to get them to outline what they see as the ways to move forward for the subject or team, and how they would like that to happen. This is where we will begin the discussion of how I can be useful in helping the school maths lead to achieve their vision, whilst also starting to gain the credibility to influence and contribute towards where that vision is heading and how it is implemented. This generally results in us being able to agree a focus for the leader and a way forward for the team, as well as helping to put the leader further at ease as they see that I am not there to impose on them but rather to work with them towards a shared goal.

Be a critical friend - but without being critical of the leader

The first two points above might make it seem as if you need to cede control of the agenda to the school maths lead. This doesn't have to be the case, but you do need to establish a balance between what you are responsible for achieving and not simply taking over the maths lead's job and leading in their stead.

A really good way to do this is to ask questions as a critical friend. Questions like: 'What makes you think that ... is the key area to focus on?' or 'Have you considered ... as an alternative approach?' are excellent examples of how to do this without rubbishing the maths lead's own ideas. There is nothing wrong with asking them to justify why they are focusing on particular aspects of practice or prompting them to consider matters they may not have brought up.

Ideally, the school maths lead should be able to answer these questions, backed up by the evidence that has led them to these conclusions. For the first question this might be: 'Our results analysis shows that ... is an area that pupils struggle with' or 'Our school and departmental quality assurance processes show that we have to do more work on ...', and for the second: 'I did consider ... but decided that ... was the better approach because ...'

When they can't do this, there is an avenue to have a conversation about these issues: 'What do we need to do to establish that ... is the key area that will lead to the improvement you want?' or 'Okay, let's consider the implications of doing ... (the alternative approach) instead of ... (the approach the maths lead initially suggested)?'

What you are doing here is building the leader's capacity; eventually, they will become used to considering these sorts of questions for themselves without the need for external prompting, and this will make them a stronger leader of their school maths team. However, at no point have you had to be critical of their current leadership approach or the suggestions they are making; you are being a critical friend without being critical of them.

Keep plenty of notes!

If you are working with a number of different schools, you will find that it can be difficult to keep track of what each school is working on and the actions that have been agreed. It can seem a little rude to make notes whilst having a conversation with a school maths lead but, again, if you are open and honest about it – simply explaining that they are for you to refer to so you can keep track of the conversations you are having with different school maths leads – then people are generally fine with this. It is a much better option than wasting time having to re-establish what you had agreed with a school maths lead each time you meet, or appearing as if you can't recall or don't know about key aspects of previous discussions.

This second point in particular is crucial as it damages your credibility (why should a school maths lead listen to you when you clearly don't know or can't remember important points you have discussed previously and therefore, it would appear, don't listen to them?) and makes it seem as if you aren't invested in the support you are offering to the school/team/lead. This sort of miscommunication will quickly sour a developing relationship with a school maths lead, and may cause irreparable harm to your ability to work with that leader or team.

Speak to the school's SLT or head teacher, but discuss this with the maths lead first

The last thing you want is for the maths lead to think you are reporting on them to the SLT. This is a sure-fire way to ensure that they are on their guard around you and stymie any hope of getting to the heart of the issues that are holding back progress with maths in the school. At the same time, clearly you are going to be having conversations with the head teacher or other members of the SLT about how your work is progressing. The best way to approach this is to be honest with the maths lead about what you are going to say when updating senior leaders, perhaps even going as far as to agree this with the maths lead. For example: 'You will understand that I have to keep the SLT informed of what we are doing. I had planned to say … Do you think this is an accurate summary of where we are at right now? Is there anything else you think I should be talking to the SLT about?' You can even go as far as to support the maths lead in addressing any concerns they may have about suggestions being made (or mandated) by the SLT that the maths lead perceives may hinder progress – again, provided you do this in a constructive way.

Part of the conversation with the head teacher or SLT might go something like: 'One of the things we [yourself and the maths lead] discussed was ... and the effect it is having. Can you tell me more about this and the impact you are hoping it will have?' Where necessary, you might be able to suggest compromises that will raise your status with the maths lead whilst also keeping the head teacher or senior team onside: 'What do you think about starting with ... and building up to ...?' or 'Do you think that ... is a suitable adaptation to ... which the maths team might be able to implement more straightforwardly?' Of course, the head or senior team could well say, 'No, we want it exactly like this,' but you still build kudos with the maths lead by asking the right questions.

Remember, you aren't there (or only rarely) to mandate a particular practice or intervention, particularly to the head teacher or senior leaders, so the key is to ask pertinent questions and listen to the answers, so you can judge how to use the results to further your aim of improving maths teaching and outcomes. It might be that you go back to the maths lead and say: 'I discussed this with your head teacher/senior team, and they want it like this because ... I did try and suggest ... and ... but they were adamant they wanted ...' This shows the maths lead that you are supportive of them and what they are aiming to achieve, and it also allows you to say something like: 'Well, given we are going to have to do ..., let's discuss how best to make this work for your team and pupils.'

You may need to be more sensitive when you are discussing what the head teacher or SLT might see as deficiencies in the maths leader or team. When first starting to work with a school, when you have relatively little information about how the intricacies of the maths lead and team work, you will probably need to speak with the head teacher or senior team to gain their perspective on the situation. When this isn't terribly positive, you will need to consider carefully what you will feed back (if anything) to the maths lead. It might be that you simply omit these details from your conversations, although it can be damaging if it later becomes known that you weren't frank with them. Sometimes it is possible to talk up the positives and use them to lessen the impact of any critical feedback.

I remember working in one school where a maths lead had been denied entry to a senior leader course by the head teacher and deputy head. The maths department had been through a period of turbulence, and whilst this was now much more settled, there were still some issues regarding staff reliability and quality. The head teacher felt that the maths lead needed to focus on transitioning the team from the firefighting past they were emerging from into the more steady state they were close to achieving, rather than splitting their focus with a whole-school project that the senior leader accreditation would require. However, the head teacher was clear that they had faith in the maths lead to manage this transition and to complete the senior lead accreditation once this period had passed.

In my initial conversation with the maths lead (I had met the head and deputy before meeting the lead), I talked up this later aspect of the conversation. The maths lead had taken their rejection from the senior leader course, and my subsequent arrival, as an indication that the head teacher didn't have faith in them. Consequently, being able to confirm absolutely that the head teacher did have belief in the maths lead's ability to move the team forward, and I was there simply to offer support (as I had previously led a team through a similar scenario in Oxford), immediately defused quite a lot of the tension the maths lead had been feeling. We ended up having a very productive time, by the end of which the maths lead was buzzing with enthusiasm for the whole process!

Leading and supporting maths across multiple schools can be a challenging and rewarding experience, particularly when you have been leading maths in a single school for a while and want to extend your skills and influence. However, it is important to remember that this is a significant responsibility and needs a meaningful investment of care, time and attention to make sure you can live up to it.

Key points

- Deal with any negative emotions that the school maths lead may have about your visit, so that you can work together successfully.
- Focus on the priorities the school maths lead has for the improvement of their team; you can steer the direction more as you build your relationship with them.
- Act as a critical friend when required, but don't be critical of the school maths lead or the team.
- Keep notes and make sure you know important details about the school maths lead, the team and what they are working on.
- Be open and honest with the school maths lead at all times, particularly around conversations you are having with the head teacher or SLT.

Chapter 13

Messages from other maths leaders

Whilst my leadership experience in maths is reasonably extensive (although I am aware there are some out there with significantly more), no one can experience everything the system has to offer. For example, I have no experience of leading in the primary or alternative provision sectors. Whilst I have worked with numerous other schools as a specialist leader of education and secondary maths mastery specialist/lead, I haven't had the responsibility and accountability that comes with having a lead role in a multi-academy trust.

The final chapter isn't mine then, but a collection of shorter case studies from colleagues whom I greatly respect who have had very different experiences from mine, and whose knowledge and expertise will add to that which I hope readers have found in this book so far.

Leading maths in a primary school

Becky Lawrence, primary school improvement lead (former primary maths lead), Success Academy Trust

Being a subject leader within a primary school is a rewarding but challenging role. In an environment where all teachers teach all subjects, often your first challenge is to make sure your subject is a priority. The advantage of leading maths is that it is a core subject and therefore it is taught every day. The national curriculum sets out very clear expectations for what is required of each year group, but it is your role as a leader to ensure these objectives are taught well and consistently in order for children to learn and make progress. The key to consistency is as simple as the three I's – intent, implementation and impact.[1]

Intent: what do you want to achieve?

As maths lead, your first step is to write your curriculum intent. This is a statement that sets out your intentions for maths and what you consider the challenges are for your school according to its context. An intent such as, 'We want our children to be passionate about maths and we want them to have high aspirations' has little impact – you would expect every school in the country to have similar values, so it is important to make your intent different. It should be meaningful, relevant and unique to meet the needs of your children in your school.

Perhaps your data shows that children begin school with a lack of reasoning skills in shape or their understanding of mathematical vocabulary is weak. Your intent will then need to specify what you are going to do to overcome these specific barriers. Questions you want to ask yourself are: 'What can your school do to make a difference in these areas?' and 'What are you going to do to change the curriculum so that you are meeting these specific needs?' It could be that you add in additional shape lessons within the early years continuous provision, or you provide additional speaking and listening activities to support children with mathematical language throughout your curriculum.

Data is a great tool to help identify these areas of strength and weakness. It should not be seen as just a way of measuring performance, but instead as an opportunity to really identify the gaps in knowledge your children have and then to help you plan actions to address them.

In addition to tailoring your curriculum, consistent pedagogy is key. How you teach is just as important as what you teach. To ensure the teaching of maths is consistent throughout the school, a maths leader needs to create long-term planning documents that show progression and coverage, and decide on a pedagogy for the subject

---

1 See Ofsted, Education Inspection Framework (updated 11 July 2022). Available at: https://www.gov.uk/government/publications/education-inspection-framework/education-inspection-framework.

and insist that it is followed without exception. Many schools use the 'Review, I do, we do, you do' approach and have very clear expectations about each step of the lesson. This is fundamental in ensuring that children receive the same standard across the school. If I am a new teacher to your school, what is it that you are expecting of me when I teach maths? Create a document or, even better, provide some one-to-one training through modelling and coaching.

Implementation: how will you achieve success?

The difference between an excellent maths teacher and an excellent maths leader is the ability to implement a plan effectively throughout the school, which means getting the buy-in of your teaching staff. This takes people skills, some of which are innate, and all of which you can develop in yourself. Insisting on a consistent approach may be the first barrier to overcome. Teachers who are particularly creative or highly experienced may be resistant to change, especially when you are telling them how you want them to teach. However, it is important that they can see the advantages of this consistent approach, whilst at the same time demonstrating a structure where individuals can bring their own style too.

Some parts of your implementation can be rolled out to staff collectively – perhaps by arranging a staff meeting and setting out the pedagogy to them. For example:

- Retention and recall are very important – do you want every lesson to start like this?
- Do you want an opportunity for children to practise new skills with equipment and resources?
- Do you want additional challenge for those children who need their thinking to be deepened, and, if so, how will this look?
- Will you use pre- or post-teach interventions?

Teaching is about individual creativity but, equally, there needs to be an expected standard. As a maths leader, you should be able to walk into a lesson and see almost immediately which part of the lesson the children are working on.

In the beginning, you will spot instances where your plan isn't being implemented as you had envisaged, so you will need to decide how and when to intervene. Firstly, don't take this personally, don't assume that your plan needs to be changed completely and don't think you aren't doing a good job. Secondly, you need to mentally accept and expect these challenges as part of the role. If you see these instances as unexpected obstacles, you will just get frustrated and demotivate yourself; overcoming disappointments is what leadership and management is all about. Coaching and mentoring, listening to staff and having a collaborative ethos is important for developing trust and buy-in in your role as a leader.

Impact: what is the outcome?

We are all measured by our results. As a teacher, additional time out of the classroom is difficult, so it can be hard to find the time to monitor your subject as closely as you would hope. It is essential that you raise this with your head teacher. You might not get more time, but there may be other things you can do that provide the feedback you need. For example, a 10-minute flick through some of the children's books after school or asking pupils what they learned that day during break duty will give you an insight into how things are going. Finding something great and something to improve is just as effective as sitting and completing a thorough book look with your school checklist. Just like children, teachers benefit from instant feedback.

As discussed already, data is a valuable tool and as a leader it can be your best friend. Data gives you the insight into how well the children are learning and remembering key concepts. Spend time on your data: identify trends, look at patterns and adapt your curriculum accordingly. Show the impact of your hard work and consider ways to improve further.

Key points

- Adapt your curriculum to meet the needs of your school community.
- Decide on a school pedagogy and insist that it is followed consistently.

- Implement the pedagogy in a way such that it will work for each individual member of your teaching staff.
- Take time to monitor the subject – sometimes less is more!
- Let data be your friend!

Leading maths across a trust

Jemma Sherwood, maths senior lead practitioner, Ormiston Academy Trust

It is very easy to be a teacher working in isolation. An isolated teacher teaches their class in the way they think is best – or the way they have always done it – with little opportunity to learn from their colleagues or share their knowledge of the craft. Without a forum for collaboration and discussion, the most (and least) fruitful of one teacher's efforts can be replicated across a department with minimal opportunity to learn from each other's successes and mistakes.

On a larger scale, the same thing can be said of mathematics departments. It is very easy to be a department in isolation. One department might have superb collective expertise in using representations to model mathematical concepts throughout the curriculum but be struggling under the weight of ineffective and time-consuming marking and assessment. Another department might have formative and summative assessment down to a fine art but have a set of A level teachers all in their first year, struggling to know where to focus their limited lesson time. Yet a third might have teachers who have taught A level for decades but who are struggling to see much progress with groups at Key Stage 3.

Just as intra-departmental collaboration can improve the coherence and quality of the mathematical experience for pupils in a school, increase teacher knowledge and skill, and reduce some aspects of workload, so inter-departmental collaboration can help us to find solutions – partial or whole – to more of the problems we face. This is where groups of schools, such as those in multi-academy trusts, can benefit.

There is no single modus operandi for a multi-academy trust. Some trusts have a central team where subject leads line manage heads of department and set the direction of departmental practices and lessons between schools. In others, the trust's subject lead allows departments to set their own priorities and focuses but oversees their progress towards these goals. I work for a trust where subject leads are responsible for centralised support and teacher development. I have a team of lead practitioners who are based in different regions of the country, each responsible for staff development across the schools in their region.

No two days are the same in the central maths team. Our schools are generally in areas of higher-than-average disadvantage, some coastal, some inner city, some rural. One day, we might be working in a school whose remote coastal location makes recruitment of maths teachers very difficult. In this school, half of the maths lessons are taught by teachers who trained in other subjects and the head of maths is new to the role. The lead practitioner coaches a PE teacher who is teaching maths for the first time and mentors the new leader, showing them how to analyse their cohort data from the latest mock to determine what interventions might be needed. At the end of the day, she models how to lead the team meeting after school where the staff have been asked to collaborate on upcoming lessons.

At the same time, across the country in an inner-city school, there is a teacher who, due to other staff leaving, has found themselves teaching A level mechanics having never done so before. The lead practitioner is there to team-teach and help with the medium-term plan and assessment writing. The same lead practitioner will be in another school the next day, where they will quality assure the curriculum at Key Stage 3 and help the head of department to get ready for inspection.

The team is building an active network of maths leaders and teachers across the trust. On top of the daily work in schools, we have half-termly meets, online and face-to-face, primary and secondary, to encourage staff to share good practice and help lighten each other's loads. We search out what is being done well and use it to inform the guidance and advice we send out to maths staff. Reading and research are an integral part of the job. We spend a lot of time growing our own knowledge of education research and the latest thinking in teaching and school improvement, then disseminating and sharing knowledge and practice between schools.

Fridays are 'national projects' day. There are lots of projects on the go, including planning for the national professional development day, where our 350 or so maths teachers will attend sessions with us on topics including using representations to build coherence from Key Stage 1 to Key Stage 5, teaching high prior attaining pupils, formative assessment in maths lessons and adapting teaching to help all pupils to access mathematics. Alongside this, we plan and deliver online sessions for early career teachers, subject knowledge enhancement for non-specialists, sessions on using particular interactive resources or concrete manipulatives, and bespoke sessions for teams in our schools when they request them.

Perhaps our most notable project is our curriculum. We are resourcing our own five-year (Year 7 to Year 11) curriculum with booklets, presentations and training materials, so that any department or teacher across the trust, no matter their level of experience or expertise, can use them as a basis for preparing their lessons. The aim is to provide a coherent curriculum baseline that reduces teachers' workload and provides ongoing professional development. Such an undertaking is complex, and the creation of materials is only part of the job. Any curricular materials, no matter how well thought-out, can live or die in the classroom. The teachers using them come to them with their own schema of mathematics and mathematics education and will, inevitably and rightly, interpret them in the light of this schema. The onus, therefore, is on our lead practitioner team to help staff understand the intent of the materials and enable them to use and adapt the materials to the greatest effect in each classroom. This means the curriculum project is inextricable from our daily work in schools.

Leading a subject, or subject development, across a trust is a varied role. Every day can look very different from the one before, more so than when working in one school. You are expected to keep abreast of developments in education and use a combination of professional learning and local knowledge to improve the standard of education across many settings. The quality of professional development you design, the curriculum resources you make, and the coaching and mentoring you provide can affect the careers of hundreds of teachers and the mathematical experiences of thousands of pupils. It is a wonderful responsibility and an important extension of the core purpose of schools – always learning, always getting better.

Key points

- Working with people is integral to the role; mentoring and coaching happen daily or weekly. Understanding the importance of development over management makes all the difference.

- Coordinating and delivering professional development requires keeping up to date with education research and thinking.

- Curriculum development and sharing of resources can happen between schools just as between classrooms, but shared resources must be adapted for each class.

- Collaboration between schools can improve the quality of education for pupils and the workload of staff. A trust lead will build a network that is beneficial to all involved.

Maths leadership

Rhiannon Rainbow, school improvement lead, and Dave Tushingham, maths lead practitioner, Greenshaw Learning Trust

As a profession we are always gaining new knowledge; this has an impact on the way we teach. In maths, subject content remains the same, but as our understanding of how we learn improves, our pedagogical approaches develop. We are constantly playing catch-up with the latest research and recommendations when designing high-quality maths and CPD curricula. Keeping this provision up to date is paramount for the success of the pupils we serve; the curriculum is never done.[2] We need to be skilled at managing the change if we are going to give our pupils the best chance of success.

The COVID-19 pandemic of 2020 posed a new challenge, forcing the education system to quickly adapt to online learning. Urgent needs arose, including the need to have access to high-quality education for pupils at home. Greenshaw Learning Trust reacted by investing significant time and resources in developing an online curriculum for a wealth of secondary subjects, including maths. Education changed overnight and teachers needed to be able to manage this

---

2   M. Myatt, Done is Better Than Perfect [blog] (14 November 2020). Available at: https://www.marymyatt.com/blog/done-is-better-than-perfect .

quickly. A team of maths teachers from across the trust were assembled to take on the role of lesson curators, who were briefed and coordinated by Rhiannon within days of closure. A very different curriculum was being intentionally designed and implemented by the team, being reviewed and refined within a very different working environment.

How we used Kotter's steps for leading change

Understanding how to manage change successfully was key to the project's success. John Kotter offers an eight-step process for leading change in his book *Leading Change*,[3] which works well as an anchor for the processes involved in making meaningful change, and we drew upon these for this project.

Our interpretation of the eight-step process for this project was:

1 Establish a sense of urgency.
2 Create the curation team.
3 Develop a vision and strategy for implementation.
4 Communication of the curriculum.
5 Empower curators.
6 Create short-term goals.
7 Consolidation of process and momentum of output.
8 Ensure effective use of the curriculum.

Step 1 was done for us through the enforced urgency of a global crisis! Teams were assembled in less than a week with a designated leader in each subject. Rhiannon's role was to form the vision alongside other leads and to communicate this to the team of maths curators. A curator would have eight lessons to make per week, starting with an online self-marking quiz of five multiple-choice questions for retrieval, then a prerequisite review. This was followed by an 'input, do, review' lesson and would finish with an online self-marking exit ticket to check for understanding. The curriculum for these lessons was sequenced differently – for example,

---

3 J. P. Kotter, *Leading Change* (Boston, MA: Harvard Business Review Press, 2012).

we avoided teaching loci in the online curriculum as pupils may not have access to specialist equipment – and we prioritised core mathematical concepts in order for it to be an accessible curriculum. Experts such as Mary Myatt[4] and Doug Lemov[5] provided expertise that supported our decision-making processes.

Rhiannon gave targets and held weekly meetings in order to review and refine goals and ensure lessons were created. Each meeting was delivered with warmth, and refined goals prepared for the next week. During the week, communication remained open if staff needed support. The lessons were made more impactful as the vision was understood and the communication was regular and consistent. The agreed goals were realistic and felt manageable in respect of helping to maintain momentum.

Whilst staff couldn't teach in the classroom, they urgently needed opportunities to grow and develop, and so a similar model was applied to our CPD curriculum. Lesson curators were already involved in excellent CPD, but the online lesson constraints forced them to work more strategically with both their language and the choice of examples used. They could practise and refine their trade in conditions where feedback was immediate and practical. This opportunity needed to be available to all, so we decided to offer high-quality CPD through a carefully sequenced set of videos. Here, staff could learn how to deliver content in key topics before being invited to practise themselves. Like the maths curriculum, key teaching skills were prioritised above others. During the lockdown, there was time to practise our explanations and delivery.

There were also opportunities for staff to delve into pedagogical theory. Less time in the classroom practising resulted in more time to acquire knowledge – for example, reading and listening to podcasts became more accessible and popular. We decided to set up a book club with the aim of supporting staff in choosing what to read or listen to; this was another significant change in the CPD teachers were used to.[6] The team working on the book club consisted of a small group of staff who met regularly. Each member of the team had a defined role, such as choosing the extract, hosting the chat, communicating with authors, sending out recordings, offering a

---

4   Myatt, Done is Better Than Perfect.
5   D. Lemov, *Teaching in the Online Classroom: Surviving and Thriving in the New Normal* (San Francisco, CA: Jossey-Bass, 2020).
6   For more information on the book club see: D. Tushingham, The First Rule of Book Club. In T. Bono (ed.), *Tiny Voices Talk: Education, Engagement, Empowerment* (Carmarthen: Independent Thinking Press, 2022), pp. 189–192.

takeaway or creating a sketchnote summary. The vision was to build a resource that could be used by teachers at all stages of their careers. As hosts, we were the constant.

Through clear, regular communication, the wider cohort of teachers were able to quickly identify and engage with the CPD that might benefit them the most. By recording and signposting further reading and key takeaways from the sessions to staff, we enabled them to extend their research. By communicating sessions every week, offering a menu of ideas and revisiting key themes, we could offer all staff opportunities to reflect on their dispositions. Reciprocated communication helped us to discover the content staff wanted to see whilst also maintaining forward momentum. We often found the CPD being used in ways and places we had not originally anticipated; this was testament to the importance of how we managed the change.

At the time of writing, both the online maths curriculum and the book club are still used. They form an important part of our continual development in the trust, and the lessons offer support for cover lessons or home learning. The book club also complements subject-specific CPD in our schools with sound bites and takeaways facilitating discussion or pedagogical ideals being taught. We see and hear about its effective use in early career teacher and SLT meetings, whole-staff and subject-specific CPD, and through informal conversations with staff.

Conclusion

Our successful adaptation to online learning was achieved through effective leadership and management of change. The key was to understand the importance of each step in the change process and apply it to both the maths curriculum and the CPD programme. The result was high-quality online maths education and ongoing professional development opportunities for teachers. The success of this endeavour serves as a model for other schools and educational organisations facing similar challenges.

Key points

- Effective leadership is crucial in managing change and adapting to new situations, such as the shift to online learning due to the global pandemic.
- Rhiannon successfully led the development of an online maths curriculum and CPD programme by following John Kotter's eight-step process for leading change and prioritising key areas for improvement.
- The provision of high-quality CPD and opportunities for personal and professional growth for teachers was emphasised, resulting in improved knowledge and delivery of maths content in the online classroom.

Summary

Whichever area or sector of education you work in, whether you already have a leadership role in maths or whether you are still looking for it, I hope the insights and experiences of myself and the other authors in this book will help to steer you through the demanding but extremely fulfilling life of a leader of mathematics teaching and education. Ultimately, there is no 'right way' to lead a subject. It will always depend on the context in which you find yourself and, like anything else, it will get easier as your experience develops all of those bits of tacit knowledge that you later rely on. However, you should always try and talk to other leaders, share your experiences and learn from theirs, and this book is perhaps one source of experience you can draw on as you navigate the world of leading maths.

References

Aguilar, E. (2012) The Power of the Positive Phone Call Home, *Edutopia* (20 August; updated 7 August 2015). Available at: https://www.edutopia.org/blog/power-positive-phone-call-home-elena-aguilar.

American University School of Education (2019) Six Highly Effective Education Leadership Styles [blog] (12 July). Available at: https://soeonline.american.edu/blog/education-leadership-styles.

Beere, J. and Broughton, T. (2013) *The Perfect (Teacher) Coach* (Carmarthen: Independent Thinking Press).

Calvert, L. (2016) The Power of Teacher Agency, *Learning Forward*, 37(2), 51–56. Available at: https://learningforward.org/wp-content/uploads/2016/04/the-power-of-teacher-agency-april16.pdf.

Carr, J. (2021) Ofsted Maths Review 'Needs to be Withdrawn', Experts Warn, *Schools Week* (9 July). Available at: https://schoolsweek.co.uk/ofsted-maths-review-needs-to-be-withdrawn-experts-warn.

Carrier, J. and Stewart, J. (2019) Episode 16: Resilience, *World of Work* [podcast]. Available at: https://worldofwork.io/2019/02/performance-and-pressure.

Christodoulou, D. (2017) *Making Good Progress? The Future of Assessment for Learning* (Oxford: Oxford University Press).

Coffey, P. (2022) Ofsted Crib Sheets Explainer: Training Guides for Ofsted Inspectors Now Free for All Schools, *Third Space Learning* (2 December). Available at: https://thirdspacelearning.com/blog/ofsted-crib-sheets.

Cunningham, M. (2019) Prioritising Subject-Specific CPD in Your School, *SecEd* (13 November). Available at: https://www.sec-ed.co.uk/best-practice/prioritising-subject-specific-cpd-in-your-school.

Darzi, A. W. (2008) *Schools: National Challenge*. HL Deb (10 June), vol. 702. Available at: https://hansard.parliament.uk/Lords/2008-06-10/debates/08061086000008/SchoolsNationalChallenge.

Department for Education (2011) *Teachers' Standards: Guidance for School Leaders, School Staff and Governing Bodies* (July; updated June 2013 and December 2021). Available at: https://assets.publishing.service.gov.uk/government/uploads/system/uploads/attachment_data/file/1040274/Teachers__Standards_Dec_2021.pdf.

Department for Education (2016) *The Link Between Absence and Attainment at KS2 and KS4: 2013/14 Academic Year. Research Report* (March). Available at: https://assets.publishing.service.gov.uk/government/uploads/system/uploads/attachment_data/file/509679/The-link-between-absence-and-attainment-at-KS2-and-KS4-2013-to-2014-academic-year.pdf.

Didau, D. (2017) Education Isn't Natural – That's Why It's Hard, *The Learning Spy* (23 February). Available at: https://learningspy.co.uk/psychology/can-learn-evolutionary-psychology.

Dix, P. (2017) *When the Adults Change, Everything Changes: Seismic Shifts in School Behaviour* (Carmarthen: Independent Thinking Press).

Durrington Research School (2021) The Hypercorrection Effect, Spaced Practice and Remote Learning (3 January). Available at: https://researchschool.org.uk/durrington/news/the-hypercorrection-effect-spaced-practice-and-remote-learning.

Engage Education (2019) Head of Department Interview Questions (8 December). Available at: https://engage-education.com/blog/head-of-department-interview-questions.

Finnis, M. (2021) *Independent Thinking on Restorative Practice: Building Relationships, Improving Behaviour and Creating Stronger Communities* (Carmarthen: Independent Thinking Press).

Guy Evans, O. (2023) Pareto Principle (The 80-20 Rule): Examples & More, *Simply Psychology* (9 February). Available at: https://www.simplypsychology.org/pareto-principle.html.

Harvard, B. (2020) Confidence Weighted Multiple-Choice Questioning, *The Effortful Educator* (22 June). Available at: https://theeffortfuleducator.com/2020/06/22/confidence-weighted-multiple-choice-questioning.

HM Government (2022) *Opportunity for All: Strong School with Great Teachers for Your Child* [white paper]. CP 650. Available at: https://www.gov.uk/government/publications/opportunity-for-all-strong-schools-with-great-teachers-for-your-child.

Hughes, H. (2021) *Mentoring in Schools: How to Become an Expert Colleague* (Carmarthen: Crown House Publishing).

Kirschner, P. A., Sweller, J. and Clark, R. E. (2006) Why Minimal Guidance During Instruction Does Not Work: An Analysis of the Failure of Constructivist, Discovery, Problem-Based, Experiential, and Inquiry-Based Teaching, *Educational Psychologist*, 41, 75–86. Available at: https://www.tandfonline.com/doi/abs/10.1207/s15326985ep4102_1.

Kornell, N. and Bjork, R. A. (2008) Learning Concepts and Categories: Is Spacing the 'Enemy of Induction'?, *Psychological Science*, 19(6), 585–592. https://doi.org/10.1111%2Fj.1467-9280.2008.02127.x

Kotter, J. P. (2012) *Leading Change* (Boston, MA: Harvard Business Review Press).

Learning Scientists (2017) Episode 8: Interleaving [podcast] (6 December). Available at: https://www.learningscientists.org/learning-scientists-podcast/2017/12/6/episode-8-interleaving.

Lemov, D. (2020) *Teaching in the Online Classroom: Surviving and Thriving in the New Normal* (San Francisco, CA: Jossey-Bass).

References

Mattock, P. (2017a) Five Ways Maths Teachers Can Persuade Secondary Colleagues to Embed Numeracy, *TES* (4 April). Available at: https://www.tes.com/magazine/archive/five-ways-maths-teachers-can-persuade-secondary-colleagues-embed-numeracy.

Mattock, P. (2017b) Ten Steps to Surviving as a New Head of Department, *TES* (21 May). Available at: https://www.tes.com/magazine/archive/ten-steps-surviving-new-head-department.

Myatt, M. (2020) Done is Better Than Perfect [blog] (14 November). Available at: https://www.marymyatt.com/blog/done-is-better-than-perfect.

National Education Union (2022) Performance-Related Pay for Teachers (25 July). Available at: https://neu.org.uk/policy/performance-related-pay-teachers.

National Research Council (2001) The Strands of Mathematical Proficiency. In *Adding It Up: Helping Children Learn Mathematics* (Washington, DC: National Academies Press), pp. 115–156. Available at: https://nap.nationalacademies.org/read/9822/chapter/6.

Northern Territory Principals' Association (2016) *A Guide to Support Coaching & Mentoring for School Improvement* (Camberwell, VIC: Australian Council for Educational Research). Available at: https://research.acer.edu.au/cgi/viewcontent.cgi?article=1012&context=professional_dev.

Ofsted (2013) School Report: Oxford Spires Academy (9–10 July). Available at: https://files.ofsted.gov.uk/v1/file/2263369.

Ofsted (2021) Research Review Series: Mathematics (25 May). Available at: https://www.gov.uk/government/publications/research-review-series-mathematics/research-review-series-mathematics.

Ofsted (2022a) Education Inspection Framework (updated 11 July). Available at: https://www.gov.uk/government/publications/education-inspection-framework/education-inspection-framework.

Ofsted (2022b) School Inspection Handbook (updated 11 July). Available at: https://www.gov.uk/government/publications/school-inspection-handbook-eif/school-inspection-handbook.

Ofsted and Spielman, A. (2019) HMCI Commentary: Managing Behaviour Research (12 September). Available at: https://www.gov.uk/government/speeches/research-commentary-managing-behaviour.

Pearson, R. (2022) Making Maths Lessons Fun – Is It the Best Way to Encourage Learning?, *Third Space Learning* (19 November). Available at: https://thirdspacelearning.com/blog/making-maths-fun-or-engaging.

Priestley, M. (2015) Teacher Agency: What Is It and Why Does It Matter?, *British Educational Research Association* (3 September). Available at: https://www.bera.ac.uk/blog/teacher-agency-what-is-it-and-why-does-it-matter.

Rosenshine, B. (2012) Principles of Instruction: Research-Based Strategies That All Teachers Should Know, *American Educator* (spring), 12–19, 39. Available at: https://www.aft.org/sites/default/files/Rosenshine.pdf.

Sheppard, E. (2021) Five Ways to Make Split Classes Work, *TES* (24 June). Available at: https://www.tes.com/magazine/teaching-learning/secondary/five-ways-make-split-classes-work.

Tushingham, D. (2022) The First Rule of Book Club. In T. Bono (ed.), *Tiny Voices Talk: Education, Engagement, Empowerment* (Carmarthen: Independent Thinking Press), pp. 189–192.

Worth, J. and Van den Brande, J. (2020) *Teacher Autonomy: How Does It Relate to Job Satisfaction and Retention?* (Slough: National Foundation for Educational Research). Available at: https://www.nfer.ac.uk/teacher-autonomy-how-does-it-relate-to-job-satisfaction-and-retention.